Prize-Winning
Quilts

The best of
2002 and
2003 shows

from the

International
Quilt Association

Rita Weiss

Sterling Publishing Co., Inc.
New York

Book design by Joyce Lerner, Graphic Solutions, Inc. – Chicago
Photos by Jim Lincoln
Photo of *3-D Party Explosion* by Sharon Risedorph

Library of Congress Cataloging-in-Publication Data Available

2 4 6 8 10 9 7 5 3 1

Published in paperback in 2006 by Sterling Publishing Co., Inc.
387 Park Avenue South, New York, NY 10016
© 2004 by The Creative Partners, LLC™
© 2004 by The International Quilt Association
Distributed in Canada by Sterling Publishing
c/o Canadian Manda Group, 165 Dufferin Street,
Toronto, Ontario, Canada M6K 3H6
Distributed in the United Kingdom by GMC Distribution Services,
Castle Place, 166 High Street, Lewes, East Sussex, England BN7 1XU
Distributed in Australia by Capricorn Link (Australia) Pty. Ltd.
P.O. Box 704, Windsor, NSW 2756, Australia

Sterling ISBN-13: 978-1-4027-2035-2 Hardcover
ISBN-10: 1-4027-2035-1
ISBN-13: 978-1-4027-4077-0 Paperback
ISBN-10: 1-4027-4077-8

For information about custom editions, special sales, premium and
corporate purchases, please contact Sterling Special Sales
Department at 800-805-5489 or specialsales@sterlingpub.com.

CONTENTS

President's Message

by JoAnn Musso, President, International Quilt Association

As president of the International Quilt Association, I am pleased to welcome you to our quilt show. You couldn't come in person, so we've brought the show to you, presenting you with the top winners from 2002 and 2003. Exhibiting these quilts in a book has been a long-held dream of ours, and we are delighted that our wish has finally materialized.

The International Quilt Association (IQA) is the only non-profit quilt association with members from around the world. Our membership is open to everyone everywhere who loves quilts. Our purposes and goals are simple:

1. To work productively toward increasing the prestige, artistry, creativity, professionalism, and recognition of quilts.

2. To foster the appreciation of quilts and quilting as an art form throughout the world and to provide necessary recognition to quilters as textile artists and to quilts as representing the mastery of textile art.

3. To unite quilters, quilt collectors, quilting teachers, retailers, and suppliers from around the world in the common goal of advancing the art and love of quilting.

4. To set and maintain the highest standards for the art of quilting, thereby encouraging further achievement within the field.

5. To offer, through a grant program, continuing education and support for the developing needs of quilters.

We hope you enjoy looking at our prize-winning quilts and reading about our fellow quilters who made the quilts. If you would like more information about IQA, or if you would like to join, you can write to us at: International Quilt Association, 7660 Woodway Drive, Suite 550, Houston, Texas 77063, or you can email us at iqa@quilts.com or visit www.quilts.org.

INTRODUCTION

BY RITA WEISS

I saw my first IQA competition and my first quilt festival in Houston in 1980. I knew how to quilt; I had been working for several years for a New York publisher, and I had edited quilt books. I arrived in Houston secure in the knowledge that there was probably nothing new that I could possibly learn about quilting.

How wrong I was!

One week later, I left the Shamrock Hilton Hotel (which was then the home base for the quilt show) in what I named "Quilt Overload," the "disease" that was to worsen over the next twenty years. The quilts became more and more amazing each year. I asked myself, "Can they get any better next year?" Each year, the answer was "Yes."

I always left Houston with the quilts embedded in my memory. But unfortunately, I could never store the memory of all the magnificent quilts I had seen. I tried to convey the splendor of a particular quilt to a friend who had not been fortunate enough to make the trip to Houston. But describing a work of art is an art in itself, and I was not a good enough artist.

For years, I have wanted to put pictures of the best quilts the International Quilt Association (IQA) has shown in their juried and judged show into a book so that I could share my appreciation with everyone. I am therefore grateful to the Board of Directors of the International Quilt Association for allowing me to do so. Special thanks are due to Past President Marti Michell, who shepherded my dream before the IQA Board, and to IQA Co-founder and Editorial Director Nancy O'Bryant and IQA *Journal* editor Bob Ruggiero who arranged the details for the photos, permission from the quilters and information for the text.

Most of all I want to thank the quilters who were willing not only to share their beautiful quilts but who took time from their busy lives to answer my probing questions about their quilting lives.

I invite you to come to Houston and to share with me the grandeur of the International Quilt Festival and the IQA Quilt Show. If you'd like more information, you can write to Quilts, Inc, 7660 Woodway, Suite 550, Houston, Texas 77063, or check out the Quilt Festival web site at www.Quilts.com.

FOREWORD

The quilts in this book were winners in "Quilts: A World of Beauty," the International Quilt Association's Judged Show of members' work, held in conjunction with the International Quilt Festival each year in Houston, Texas. The Festival, inspiration of Karey Patterson Bresenhan, a fifth generation Texas quilter, provides the annual showcase for what is one of the world's largest judged quilt shows.

In 1974, Karey, the first female vice president outside New York City at a prestigious international public relations firm, felt she could make a difference by entering public life. She decided to start her political career by running for the Texas Legislature. She won a tough primary, triumphing over the old-boy network in place at the time, but winning the general election proved to be daunting. It wasn't until after she had lost the election that she learned her chances had been slight indeed. It seems that, out of the entire country, her district historically was one of the most firmly ensconced in the opposing party's camp.

Karey had raised money for her campaign by holding meetings in the homes of friends. Although debts incurred in running for public office are frequently forgiven, Karey was determined to pay her debts to family and friends. She and her mother-in-law decided that they would try the antique business, with Karey planning to use her proceeds from the store to repay the debt. The only available location they could find had at one time been a huge pet shop, and the antiques they had to sell, when scattered around, scarcely filled the space. The walls looked quite bare and foreboding. Ever resourceful, however, the women hit upon an idea to make the shop more inviting. Because Karey's family had been making quilts for generations, there were plenty of family quilts at home. The women brought out the quilts – not to sell – but to decorate the shop and cover its bare walls. With high hopes, they named it Great Expectations.

Customers who came to the shop, however, found the quilts to be much more enticing than the antiques. Farewell to the antique business! Karey bought out her mother-in-law, and Great Expectations became a quilt shop, remaining one of the top quilt stores in the country for the next 29 years.

At the close of her first year in business, Karey held a thank-you party at her shop for her loyal customers. She invited Bryce and Donna Hamilton, well-known quilt experts, to lecture and bring their wares, including rare Old Order and Midwest Amish quilts. The party, a precursor to International Quilt Festival, was a huge success. Over 2500 people attended, many standing in the rain and waiting patiently to get into the store, where over $20,000 of the Hamilton's quilts were sold.

In the next few years the Festival outgrew facilities at the River Oaks Garden Club and gymnasiums at both St. Paul's and St. Luke's Methodist churches in Houston. In 1980, the Festival moved to the Shamrock Hilton Hotel, where it stayed for eight years until the hotel was sold and eventually torn down. During those years, the quilters at International Quilt Festival completely filled the hotel, turning it into a giant slumber party each night, with quilters in pajamas drinking coffee and stitching in the lobby until all hours. For a year after the demise of the Shamrock, Festival held forth in the Albert Thomas Convention Center, until it became the first public show at the new George R. Brown Convention Center, where it has stayed with only one year's foray to the Astrohall.

As the interest in quilting continued to grow, the International Quilt Festival did also. It is now the largest convention in Houston, the nation's fourth largest city.

HOW IQA BEGAN

In 1979, few quilting organizations existed on other than a local level. Karey and her mother, Jewel Pearce Patterson, her aunt, Helen Pearce O'Bryant, and her cousin, Nancy O'Bryant, had a vision of an organization that would be a bit different from those then in place. They wanted to create an organization whose mission would be to spread the love of quilting, not remain primarily a club for people who were already involved in the activity. They started the South/Southwest Quilt Association (S/SWQA), which by the end of the year had a grand total of 127 members. It was their plan to reach out to enlist new devotees, not to "preach to the choir." They believed in quilting as an art that deserved respect and that educating people about quilts and quilting was the best way to achieve that recognition and further its acceptance beyond local communities.

The Founders (left to right): Karey Bresenhan, Nancy O'Bryant, Jewel Patterson, Helen O'Bryant

When S/SWQA was started, there was something of a bias against people who made their living in some aspect of the quilting field. People who sold supplies, who taught, or who ran quilt shops were considered by some to be less "pure" in their love of quilts and quilting. The South/Southwest Quilt Association was created to be all-inclusive. The founders wanted this to be an open organization that would welcome anyone who loved quilts, whether they actually made them or not. Collectors, designers, teachers, authors, pattern makers, notions inventors, quilt researchers, suppliers, shop owners, textile conservators, and publishers of magazines and quilt books all were invited to participate on an equal basis with quiltmakers in helping to preserve and advance the art.

The following year, members received the premiere issue of the group's journal, the *South/Southwest Quiltmaker,* now a four-color magazine known as

Quilts. . .A World of Beauty. The first Judged Show of members' quilts was held in conjunction with the general membership meeting, the Lone Star Quilt Conference, at International Quilt Festival. In 1982, the first Board of Directors was inducted, with Judy Murrah as President. Over the years, eleven other members would move into the presidency, including, in alphabetical order: Georgia Bonesteel, Karen Kay Buckley, Linda Fiedler, Helen Young Frost, Irma Gail Hatcher, Marti Michell, JoAnn Musso, Jean Roberts, Rita Weiss, Gerry Wilkinson, and Lynn Lewis Young. Membership continued to increase, and by 1983 an official membership pin was created and presented to all members.

The rest of the 1980s saw continued progress and growth in all aspects of the organization. It was recognized as a 501(c)(3) not-for-profit entity. A Grant Program, still an integral part of IQA today, was introduced to offer financial support to qualified, worthy quilt projects and quilters. This is an important part of the educational mission of IQA and is one of its proudest achievements. Grants go for such diverse projects as one to the University of Nebraska-Lincoln for a study on fusibles called "The Effects of Light and Ageing on Selected Quilting Products and Adhesives" to another awarded to a member who ships monthly packages containing quilting supplies to a group of 17 quilters in the Republic of Georgia, one of the former Soviet Union republics. That project is helping to spread the love and appreciation of quilting around the world, another of IQA's stated goals.

Soon after its founding, the South/Southwest Quilt Association discovered that its membership included quilters from Southern California, Southwestern Chile, Southern Vermont, and Southwestern Canada, to note only a few such areas. In 1985, the group changed its name to the American/International Quilt Association (AIQA), and counted its membership at well over 1000. Although the organization began to have a strong international flavor, members at that time wanted to keep the word "American" to commemorate the birthplace of the organization.

To celebrate the Texas state sesquicentennial in 1986, and to raise funds for AIQA, the four Texas founders collaborated on *The Founders Star,* an original feathered five-pointed star medallion quilt. Kathleen McCrady, a charter member of the organization, won it and generously donated it to the founders three years later. It now hangs in Houston, where IQA has its office.

1988 proved to be a monumental year for the international part of the name as the AIQA sponsored the first international Quilt Expo, held in Salzburg, Austria. It was a definite turning point in spreading both the group's message and quilting beyond the shores of the United States. Membership at the time had risen to more than 2,000 members.

Quilt Expo (now Patchwork & Quilt Expo) remains one of the most important accomplishments of IQA. The first Expo was a magical time for quilters throughout the world. No one present will ever forget it; something special had transpired at that first Roll Call of the Nations. AIQA, as the sponsoring organization, had the vision and the courage to be involved with something totally different. In the ensuing years, the biennial Quilt Expo has been held in Austria (twice), Denmark, The Netherlands (twice), Germany, France (twice), and Spain.

A DECADE OF GROWTH

The 1990s saw an era of unprecedented growth both in the quilting world and the organization. More categories were added to the Judged Show, which began offering corporate-sponsored cash prizes to winners in 1996, befitting its status as one of the most prestigious quilt contests in the world. Since the awards were not purchase prizes, quilters received the recognition, the money, and kept their work of art. That same year, the group changed its name yet again to better reflect its membership and its goals, to the International Quilt Association (IQA). Membership continues to grow today, surpassing 5000 members in well over 30 countries.

WHAT MEMBERSHIP MEANS

IQA members receive benefits far beyond membership pins, cards, and quarterly journals. They get a chance to participate in the enlightenment of the general public about quilts, and are offered the opportunity to exhibit their best work for the world to see, raising standards for the art and educating viewers at the same time. More than 50,000 people from all over the globe arrive at the annual International Quilt Festival in Houston each year to appreciate the IQA Judged Show entries and to learn about the organization and its educational mission from volunteers.

IQA participates in various oral history and documentation efforts to spread interest in the history of quiltmaking in the 20th and 21st centuries, such as the Boxes Under the Bed™ and Quilters' SOS: Save Our Stories projects spearheaded by The Alliance for American Quilts. IQA is also involved in continuing education through jointly sponsored activities such as the 1998 Appraisal Seminar at the International Quilt Festival, in cooperation with The Alliance and the Studio Art Quilt Associates. In 1999, IQA participated in "The Ultimate Quilt Search" to identify the Twentieth Century's 100 Best American Quilts as one of four non-profit organizations invited to nominate selectors who chose the quilts so honored. Those quilts were presented in a special exhibit and book at International Quilt Festival in 1999.

Jewel Pearce Patterson, one of the four founders, died in 2002 at the age of 92. The other three founders continue to be active in IQA and continue to judge their $7500 Founders Award, sponsored by International Quilt Festival. The Founders Award is given each year to a member's quilt that best expresses traditional values in quiltmaking.

IQA TODAY

Over the next few years, the main goals of IQA will include increasing its international membership and coordinating more exhibits like those the organization sponsors at selected venues in the U.S. and abroad. Now the largest non-profit international quilt organization in the world, IQA continues to thrive and grow due to the creativity and dynamism of its elected board and the interest and enthusiasm of its diverse and far flung membership.

THE JUDGED SHOW

In 1980 at the first IQA (then called S/SWQA) show, all quilts entered in the competition were hung. The unofficial motto was, "You enter 'em; we'll hang 'em." The judge arrived just in time to do the judging, and the ribbons were placed upon the quilts.

As soon as the doors opened, eager quilters rushed into the room where the quilts were displayed to learn whether or not they had been awarded a prize. Prior to 1996, a win meant a ribbon and the "greater glory".

Times change, and the competition has changed as well. Today the judges meet about a month before the show with the judging often taking several days. A gala Winners Circle Celebration often referred to by many as "The Quilting Oscars" is a highlight of the multi-media awards ceremony. The awards today are cash prizes, as well as ribbons, including the following:

The Best of Show	$10,000
The Founders Award	$7,500
The Master Awards	$5,000
Judge's Choice Awards	$250
Viewers' Choice Award	$500
Category Awards	
First Place	$1,000
Second Place	$700
Third Place	$300

In the late 90s the board of the IQA reached the decision that there were too many quilts entered to hang at the show, and that the entries would have to be juried. This made the competition even keener as each quilt entered had been invited. A preliminary three-member panel, chosen by the board of directors, reviews the quilts through photographs and slides. The jury for the 2003 show included Judy Mathieson, Stevii Graves, and Sally Davey. They reviewed 826 entries and juried it down to 408 finalists. In 2002, Marilyn Dorwart, Sandra Donabed, and Teddy Pruett looked at 755 entries to reach the 441 finalists.

The judges for the 2003 competition, again chosen by the board, were: Liz Axford, Nancy Brenan Daniel, and Dixie McBride. The judges for the 2002 competition were: Pepper Cory, Cynthia England and Joen Wolfrom. The judge for the wearable art category for both years was JoAnn Musso.

2003 Best of Show:
1776 – Heartache, Heritage
and Happiness

Pussycat-Pussycat,
Where Have You Been?

LIZ AXFORD, HOUSTON, TEXAS

Liz Axford began quilting seriously in 1986. At that time she was a practicing architect, and she saw in quilting the ability to explore design problems similar to those in architecture using new materials and involving greater freedom.

Since 1987 her quilts have won top prizes at many prestigious shows including several awards at IQA shows. She was the winner of the Quilt Japan Prize at Visions in San Diego. She has judged many shows including the 1999 IQA Show and juried the 2002 Quilt National Show.

She insists that a prize-winning quilt needs to be visually fresh and technically excellent. She believes that the quilts in the IQA competition improve constantly in design and technique with each passing year.

She chose *Pussycat-Pussycat, Where Have You Been?* by Lorraine Carthew as her Judge's Choice because she loves her own cats, and these cats, she felt, were not only well drawn, but charming and sympathetic to the medium – that is, more quilterly than painterly. Liz is just dopey for cats.

"I wish quiltmakers would improve their technical skills," she writes. "There are too many art quilts of stunning visual impact, but disappointing, or short on workmanship. While a winning quilt must have more than good workmanship, the workmanship should not detract from the enjoyment of the visual effect. Quilts that are made to sell should be made to last."

NANCY BRENAN DANIEL, TEMPE, ARIZONA

Nancy Brenan Daniel has enjoyed quilting her entire adult life. She loves writing, designing and teaching hand quilting, appliqué, color and design, and rotary techniques.

Her love of quilts came from her grandmother who encouraged her to play with fabrics and quilts at a very young age. She started her first quilt when she was ten or twelve. She feels that her interest in quilts and quilting drew her closer to her grandmother and to the other women in her family.

Active in the quilt world for many years as a teacher and designer, Nancy is also the author of more than 20 books on sewing crafts and quiltmaking. Although quiltmaking and design currently take up much of her time, she continues to travel, to teach and to judge. She has judged at the AQS show twice, and judged shows for the National Quilters Association as well as many state, guild, and symposium quilt shows from coast to coast since 1985.

While each quilt show category will have its own set of criteria, and Nancy tries to follow those, there are certain basics that she feels are her criteria for a prize-winning quilt. She looks for a quilt that is well made; with strong unified design elements, a personal approach to an idea by the quilter, and an unusual or unexpected twist presented by the quilter.

Touch Tone Dilemma by Charlotte Patera was Nancy's Judge's Choice. She feels that it is a unique, small quilt. Its theme – and title – is one that humans can almost universally respond to. According to Nancy, art and fine quilts reach out and touch universal themes; they cross cultural borders easily. The humor and angst delivered by this quilt can be understood by anyone with a telephone.

"Most winning quilts," writes Nancy, "are the result of quilters who cast about in their lives and studios for personal choices in fabrics, techniques, and themes. Winning quilts originate with quilters who have a personal vision and who are willing to take chances in their creation. My message to all quilters is to experiment, take chances, make personally rewarding quilts."

Touch Tone Dilemma

DIXIE MCBRIDE, EUREKA, CALIFORNIA

Dixie McBride has been sewing since childhood. She began quilting in 1978 following "the fad" at the time. Over the years her style in quiltmaking developed. Mastery of the needle has made her a popular teacher of technical and creative classes. Her unaffected warmth and supportive teaching style is effective in stretching a student's natural abilities. She brings to life individuality along with refining techniques. Dixie is the recipient of numerous top national and international awards and regularly contributes to quilting publications. She is a judge and juror for top-level competitions.

Her quilts have earned over 100 awards including a Best of Show at IQA. Her quilt *Peacocks* was honored as runner-up in the Twentieth Century's 100 Best American Quilts.

Dixie's criteria for a prize-winning quilt are design, proper use of color, mature composition, and technical skills. She feels that it does not matter if the quilt is in a traditional or innovative category. For her, the quilt that takes the prize must be unique and/or masterful in its execution.

She chose as her Judge's Choice Quilt *Kimberly Mystique* by Gloria Loughman because the subject matter was unique and original, exhibiting a beautifully artistic interpretation of nature's Boab trees. The workmanship, she felt, was superior and

Kimberly Mystique

during the judging process this quilt kept calling her back saying, "Show me to the world."

"It was an honor," Dixie writes, " to be selected as one of the judges for the IQA show. Diligence and scrutiny are a judge's constant companions while examining the many top quality quilts this show attracts. Many of the quilts very easily could have been chosen as the winners and those not chosen should not discourage the artists from future competitions."

2003 JUDGES

2002 JUDGES

2002 Best of Show:
Flowers of the Crown

PEPPER CORY, MOREHEAD CITY, NORTH CAROLINA

Pepper Cory began quilting when she was a nineteen-year old "hippie chick". She thought that she needed to know all the back-to-earth skills. Quilting won out over soap making, weaving, canning her own food, and shearing sheep.

After years of study and even operating her own quilt shop, Pepper began teaching and sharing her love of quilting with quilters all over the world. She has written numerous books and articles and has designed stencils and fabric. In 2002, she was the winner of the Jewel Pearce Patterson Award, presented to quilt teachers. The award includes a trip to Patchwork and Quilt Expo (for American teachers) or to International Quilt Festival (for international teachers).

Pepper does not enter competitions, but she has organized a number of exhibitions of her works, and she has judged at other quilt competitions.

Although each show has unique judging guidelines, Pepper tries to align her personal likes and dislikes with these criteria. In her opinion a prize-winning quilt has to have what she calls the "One-Two-Three Punch." Number One: the piece has to have graphic appeal. Number Two: the workmanship must be excellent. Number Three: artistically the piece should contain balance and display merit.

Pepper feels that the Judge's Choice Award is a completely subjective category. She simply asked herself, "Which quilt would I love to own." She gave her Judge's Choice Award to *The Sexagenary Cycle* by Taeko Ohya because the concept of the quilt was charming, and the animals of the Chinese Zodiac were well portrayed and beautifully executed. She simply fell in love with the quilt.

Pepper remembers the Awards Ceremony at which she announced her Judge's Choice win. "The quiltmaker spoke no English," writes Pepper, "but timidly came up the aisle to receive her award bowing to everybody right and left. When she got on stage, I handed her the bouquet and said, 'From someone who was born in the Year of the Rabbit, many thanks for sharing this lovely quilt with us.' Then I bowed, lower than she did, to indicate my great respect for her work. We were both a little teary-eyed after that!"

CYNTHIA ENGLAND, HOUSTON, TEXAS

Cynthia England actually began quilting at the age of 13, but her interest was rekindled again in 1976 during the Bicentennial. Essentially a self-taught quilter, she has completed at least 24 bed-sized quilts and over 70 wall quilts. Although she started with traditional quilts, Cynthia today is known for her realistically detailed pictorial quilts. After using appliqué to get her effects, she gradually devised a machine piecing technique she calls "Picture Piecing".

The first quilt she made, using this effect, *Piece and Quiet,* won a Best of Show at the 1993 IQA show and was named one of the Twentieth Century's 100 Best American Quilts. She won a second Best of Show for her *Open Season* in 2000.

Judging quilts since 1998, she looks for visual impact and good proportions of design elements. She is especially taken with anything out of the ordinary, whether unusual combinations of blocks, sets, color choices, or a variety of techniques. For Cynthia the design has to flow and move her eyes throughout the quilt; the colors have to work together, and the techniques chosen must be well executed.

Graven Images by Judy Coates Perez was her Judge's Choice. Cynthia's interest in family history leads her to find old tombstones and graveyards intriguing. She felt that the quilter had found a way to put these ideas into a beautiful quilt. The workmanship she found to be fabulous and the color choices perfect. It was a quilt that spoke to her.

"Judging quilts," writes Cynthia, "is a difficult job. It is not an exact science. Each judge approaches the task differently. I would encourage every quilter to enter quilt shows. Every time I have entered quilt shows, and the comments come back, they were things that I knew in the back of my mind that could have been improved. That information helped me in making my next quilt. Each and every year I am amazed at what the talented quilters come up with. Quilting truly is an art form."

The Sexagenary Cycle

Graven Images

Joen Wolfrom , Fox Island, Washington

Joen Wolfrom began quilting in 1973 when she bought matching fabric for the wallpaper in her baby daughter's bedroom. She wanted to make a simple quilt. While she knew how to sew, she didn't know how to quilt. The result was deplorable! Soon after, she took an evening class at the local high school. The teacher gave her students a new project every week, highlighting a different technique or style. At the end of twelve weeks, Joen had eleven unfinished projects. She took the class three times just to finish the projects.

Since then Joen has left the education field, where she had been an elementary teacher and a consultant in special and gifted education, to become a full time quilt instructor, lecturer, author, quiltmaker, pattern designer and the owner of her own pattern company.

Although she won prizes in quilt competitions in the 70s, 80s and early 90s, Joen no longer enters her quilts in competitions. Receiving an award has never been a goal for her. She makes quilts to please her soul and to challenge her abilities. She usually judges about three shows per year, and has served as a judge for both IQA and Visions.

Cassandra Williams's *River Run* was Joen's Judge's Choice Award. The quilt also ended up winning a First Place in the Pictorial Quilt Category although Joen usually selects a quilt for Judge's Choice that has not received one of the major awards

River Run

in the show. She felt that this quilt was unusually beautiful, and it truly spoke to her. Being from salmon country she knew that Cassandra's interpretation of salmon was stunning, and she felt that the visual depth and colors of the salmon were superb. In making a Judge's Choice award, Joen looks for a quilt that incorporates good use of design and color, with an all-encompassing technique. Finally the quilt should pique her interest in some way. She finds herself giving the award to a quilt that compels her to come back to it repeatedly. She felt that Cassandra did an extraordinary job of using her fabrics to create the fleeting iridescence of the salmon.

Joen has noted that in the last few years, quilts given the highest accolades by quilters often use more than one technique. Sometimes a quilt appears to have a better chance at winning an award when it combines techniques such as piecing and appliqué. She feels, however, that giving awards to these quilts is not a conscious decision by judges. Instead it merely emphasizes the fact that well-blended techniques can create visually exquisite quilts.

"I believe technical skill is important," writes Joen. "However, I realize it is unrealistic to insist that a quilter should make a perfect quilt. There are days when one's hands, body, or mind just refuse to comply with perfection. So, I look for consistently good workmanship. I try not to demand perfection; however, the best-of-show quilt should be one of the most exquisitely made quilts. The combination of technique and design should be better than every other quilt in the show. Shirley Kelly's *Flowers of the Crown* was awesome. Her workmanship was unbelievable. The illusions of depth and lighting were excellent. Everything about this quilt was exquisite. Although there were other wonderful quilts in this show, Shirley's stood out in design, technique, and creativity.

"Our large quilt exhibits and shows are filled with amazing quilts. The award winners are awesome. This particular show seems to motivate many people to create quilts to their highest potential. I am in awe of so many of the quilters whose works we see in the International Quilt Association Show."

2003 & 2002 WEARABLE ART JUDGE

JoAnn Musso, Dallas, Texas

JoAnn Musso, the newly elected president of the International Quilt Association, has been sewing and designing wearables for 45 years. In 1990, she attended her first Quilt Festival, and that experience dramatically changed her life. She began to teach and lecture on her embellishment techniques for wearable art.

JoAnn has taught and judged at major shows around the United States. She has made garments for both the Fairfield and the Bernina Fashion Shows, and her garments have won awards, and have been sold in galleries and exhibited both here and abroad.

In addition to her wearable art, JoAnn does make quilts. She made her first quilt in 1999 as a graduation gift for her granddaughter. She used a magazine pattern to make a *Texas Lone Star,* and she appliquéd violets in a circle on the star and in the borders. That first quilt appears in the *ABC's of Quilting* by Bonnie Browning.

When JoAnn judges a garment she looks for excellent workmanship, fashionable design, and wearability.

2003:
Putting On
the Ritz

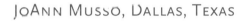

2002:
Mainbocher

2003 QUILTS

1776 – HEARTACHE, HERITAGE AND HAPPINESS

by Pam Holland, Aldgate, South Australia

100" x 110" (254cm x 279cm) Machine pieced and machine quilted

"I found a picture of this quilt some eight years ago. I was constantly drawn to the quilt and in 1999, with trepidation, I decided to reproduce it. I traveled around the world to Bautzen, a 1000-year-old walled city in East Germany, and located the original quilt, which was made by Sorbian soldiers from their woolen uniforms. In October 2001, my obsession was rewarded by discovering that my family were Sorbian and had lived in Bautzen for some 500 years before migrating to Australia."
– Pam Holland

Pam Holland, a fashion designer and a photographer, walked into a quilt shop in Australia in 1991 and was intrigued. She had worked with fabrics for many years, and suddenly she realized that she could use fabrics in a creative way for pure pleasure. Her first quilt, a traditional sampler with a few additions, remains folded in her "precious" file. One day she plans to use it to grace the bed it was intended for, but for now she's much too busy garnering awards at quilt shows throughout the world, from Yokohama, Japan to Duluth, Minnesota,

This prize-winning quilt has been a large part of Pam's life for the past eight years. She estimates that she has spent over 9,596 hours creating her masterpiece. She reproduced the quit using reproductions of fabrics produced in 1776; however modern sewing machines for piecing and appliqué techniques were used. Creating the quilt was therapy for working through the death of one of her children. She and her husband are parents to thirteen children, three biological and ten adopted from overseas. In addition, they have been parents to 150 foster children.

Winner of the 2001 Jewel Pearce Patterson Scholarship for International Quilt Teachers, Pam travels all over the world teaching. She counts herself very lucky to be involved in the quilting industry which has allowed her to share her knowledge and her love with thousands of wonderful people. She enjoys a passion for antique quilts and their method of construction. In the future she wants to study quilts as cultural documents and introduce her students to the forgotten techniques associated with the art of quilting.

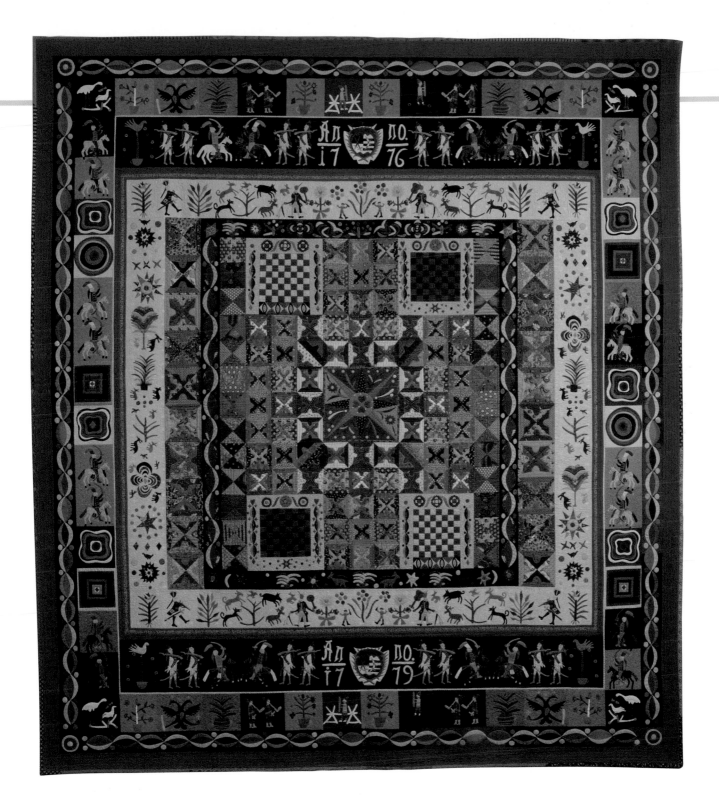

SUNSHINE ROSE GARDEN

By Yachiyo Katsuno. Setagaya, Tokyo, Japan

90" x 91" (229cm x 231cm) Hand pieced, hand appliquéd and hand quilted

"I made this quilt as an expression of the best patch-work quilt I could do. I added the rose motifs because I felt it needed something besides red piecing work. The most difficult part was to arrange the color of the appliquéd flowers. It made me wonder how I could balance the colors with the red pieced parts. I became full of energy doing this work from beginning to end."
– Yachiyo Katsuno

Yachiyo Katsuno is probably best known in Japan by her professional name, Kathy Nakajima. In Japan she is a TV personality and a member of the national morning TV show. She commutes every week by train to Nagoya where she hosts a radio talk show, and she quilts on the train.

Her TV career began early; she was a cast member of a Charlie's Angels type TV show that predated the American version by several years. She was a model for print ads and TV, and has published over 30 books on various lifestyle topics including cooking and quilting.

Her husband, Hiroshi Katsuno, is also a TV personality, and her three children are joining the family business of lifestyles, TV and quilting. Her new magazine *Kathy Mom* features the family engaging in fashion, cooking, crafts and quilting.

Her quilting life began over thirty years ago when she discovered an old quilt in a shop in Los Angles that reminded her of a quilt she had seen in the movie *Little Women*. Today in addition to her TV work, she is an accomplished quilter with three quilt stores in the Tokyo area in which quilting classes are offered. Through her company, Studio K, she not only trains authorized teachers throughout Japan but also offers a correspondence course on video or DVD. She makes several trips to the United States every year to purchase specialty fabrics; she is probably one of the largest purchasers of the hand-dyed fabrics from Shades, many of which can be seen in her prize-winning quilt.

ALABASTER RELIEF

By Zena Thorpe, Chatsworth, California

74" x 86" (180cm x 218cm) Hand quilted

"This quilt was inspired by a plasterwork ceiling in Knole House in Kent, England. The effect is of an alabaster carving with serpentine ribs and shallow relief botanical emblems."

– Zena Thorpe

A member of The Master Quilters Guild (one of only 17 members in the United States), Zena Thorpe is one of today's outstanding quilters. Her *Kells: Magnum Opus,* was named a Masterpiece Quilt by the National Quilting Association. Her *Crowned with Glory-Right Royally,* which won the Founder's Award in the 1996 IQA competition, was named one of the Twentieth Century's 100 Best American Quilts.

Referred to by *Quilter's Newsletter Magazine* as "one of 30 distinguished quilt makers of the world," Zena has been quilting for over 25 years ago. A friend who taught quilting encouraged her to try a Log Cabin quilt, but it was when Zena discovered appliqué that her real interest in quilting was born.

Her quilts have won major awards both in the United States and overseas. Her quilt, *Frogmore* won both a Founders Award and a Best of Show at the 1994 IQA competition. *To England with Love* won the National Patchwork Championship in England in 1990 in addition to winning awards both at the IQA and AQS competitions.

Out of the Strong Came Forth Sweetness was the Viewers' Choice at the World Quilt 2000 competition in addition to being named Champion Quilt at the 1999 Scottish Quilt Championships.

Married and the mother of four children, Zena trained and worked as a medical research assistant, but today her only pastime is quilting. She labored diligently for over one year to complete this prize-winning quilt.

PATIO SCENE II, SUNDAY©

By Jean M. Evans, Medina, Ohio

78" x 87" (198cm x 221cm) Machine pieced, machine quilted, hand appliqué, and hand painting

"Large hand painted and hand appliquéd graphic shapes. Plain and printed fabrics and splashed-on color invite a relaxing day on the patio."

– Jean M. Evans

Winning prizes at the International Quilt Festival has become a habit for Jean Evans; her *Sun on Marty's Bike©*, which appears on page 109, earned the first place award in the Art Quilt Small category in 2002.

In 1976 during a week-long snowstorm, Jean was searching for something to pass the time. She knew nothing about quiltmaking, but she had sewn clothing and things for her home for many years. There was an abundance of fabric in her house, and a neighbor, who had a collection of her mother's old quilt patterns, was willing to share. She sewed a few blocks and decided that this was fun. By the time the ice and snow had melted, she had finished a sampler bed size quilt, and had become a quilter for life.

It didn't take long, however, for her to decide that it would be much more enjoyable to design her own quilts. Today Jean experiences the joy and creative pleasure as well as the struggle and frustration that accompanies that decision. She is influenced more by what she experiences and she imagines than by what is being done by other quilt makers.

Jean worked on this quilt for over a year.

THE PFAFF MASTER AWARD FOR
MACHINE ARTISTRY
AWARD SPONSORED BY
PFAFF SALES AND MARKETING

THE SPACE QUILT

By Sue Nickels and Pat Holly, Ann Arbor, Michigan

88" x 88" (224cm x 224cm) Machine pieced and machine quilted

"This completely machine stitched quilt pays tribute to the U.S. space program. Our father was an Air Force fighter pilot in WWII and we watched all space launches culminating in the first man on the moon. NASA and space exploration are so important to our future. We hope our quilt gives a chance to look back at the past and forward to our final frontier."

— Sue Nickels and Pat Holly

Sue Nickels and Pat Holly are quiltmaking partners and sisters who started quilting about 25 years ago, teaching themselves and taking classes at local shops. They began quilting by hand and gradually began focusing on machine work. They make their own quilts, but every other year they combine their creative talents and work on a quilt together.

The first quilt they made together was a *Dresden Plate* style which was intended as a gift for their mother. They so enjoyed working together that a decision was made to continue their joint effort. Their next quilt, *Blackbirds Fly,* won several awards including a third place in group quilts at the 1996 AQS show. In 1998 their third joint project, *The Beatles Quilt,* took the Best of Show honors at the 1998 AQS show.

The sisters also have co-authored a number of books on machine quilting patterns, and have worked together as contributing editors for *Ladies Circle Patchwork Quilts Magazine.* They find it very rewarding to work together, honoring the tradition of quilting together with friends and family.

Sue and Pat especially loved working on *The Space Quilt* because it was a tribute to their dad who died unexpectedly on Christmas Day, 2003. He was able to see this wonderful quilt and to know about the great award it received. This has made this quilt even more special for the sisters.

A VEIL FOR HIMIKO

By Yoriko Nose, Niigata-shi, Niigata, Japan

70" x 72" (178cm x 178cm) Machine pieced and machine quilted

"Himiko is the name of a Japanese Queen from the early third century. The old mysterious story about her inspired me; therefore, I invented this technique and chose Japanese primitive patterns. This is a double-faced quilt – the front means glory, and the back means innocence."

– Yoriko Nose

After graduating from a design school in Tokyo Yoriko began working as a designer, but soon found quilting to be an interesting challenge. Inspired by looking at other people's quilts, she began making quilts herself.

Today her quilts have won prizes in many Japanese exhibits including a Gold Prize in the Quilt Nihon Exhibition in May, 2001.

Her *A Veil for Himiko* took eight months to complete and is based upon the legend that surrounds the historical Himiko. The legend tells the tale of an empress who never made an appearance before a crowd; her younger brother conveyed her orders. Attended by 1,000 maids, Himiko never married, and to this day her grave stands unspoiled as a reminder of her immaculate life. The story haunted Yoriko and inspired her to construct this quilt in Himiko's memory. When the quilt won this award, Yoriko felt that Himiko herself was responsible for the honor

PUSSYCAT-PUSSYCAT, WHERE HAVE YOU BEEN?

By Lorraine Carthew, Teneriffe, Brisbane, Australia

"The appliquéd mosaic design depicting two cats in the garden was done using needle turn appliqué. This is a new form of appliqué I have been developing over the last two years."

– Lorraine Carthew

59 3/4" x 70 3/4" (152cm x 180cm) Hand pieced and machine quilted

Although Lorraine Carthew's husband refers to quilting as an "all consuming hobby," for Lorraine it is an "all consuming" form of artistry that complements her background in fabric and fashion design. In addition to this Judge's Choice Award at the IQA show, Lorraine's quilts have won prizes at the Queensland Quilt Show, the New South Wales Quilt Show, the RNA Quilts Across Queensland Show and the World Quilt and Textile Competition. *PussyCat-PussyCat, Where Have You Been?* took approximately 12 months to complete.

Lorraine started quilting 8 years ago and it was a natural progression after years of needlework. Her broad experience with color-washing has formed the backdrop of her many award-winning quilts. Many of Lorraine's quilts use two techniques that she has pioneered, the "Mosaic Technique" used on this award-winning quilt and the "Portrait Technique" which has been used for many of her Australian award-winners. Lorraine sees herself as a quilting and textile artist; her many "viewers' choice" awards attest to the integrity of her quilting artistry.

TOUCH TONE DILEMMA

By Charlotte Patera, Grass Valley, California

53" x 50" (135cm x 127cm) Machine pieced, machine quilted, and hand computer printed appliqué

"Who in the civilized world has not known the frustration of the automated answering machine with a menu of options that do not apply to your call and with no human being available? Sometimes it is difficult to know what to press next."
— Charlotte Patera

Charlotte Patera was a graphic designer in Chicago and San Francisco for well-known industrial designers for over twenty years. In the 1970s she began designing needlecraft projects for national magazines including *Better Homes and Gardens, Family Circle, Woman's Day* and *Good Housekeeping*. She decided to concentrate on quilting because she felt it offered the most creativity. She made her first quilt in 1973 for a book on appliqué for *Better Homes and Gardens.*

Early in her appliqué work, Charlotte became intrigued with the mola work of the Kuna Indians of Panama. She returned to Kuna Yala on the San Blas Islands of Panama seven times in order to collect their work, learn their methods, and observe their lifestyle. Much of her work has been inspired by these molas, and she has taught this technique throughout the world.

Today her quilts number well over a hundred; she has written five books and many magazine articles, and her quilts are featured in various prestigious art collections. Her work has been exhibited in major exhibitions including Quilt National. In 2003, three of her quilts were shown in Tokyo as part of an exhibit of the Thirty Distinguished Quilt Artists of the World.

KIMBERLEY MYSTIQUE

By Gloria Loughman, Kerang, Victoria, Australia

78" x 82" (198cm x 211cm) Machine pieced, machine quilted

"The challenge of traveling to the wilderness of the Kimberley is rewarded by the sight of the mystical Boab Trees. Each specimen has a unique appearance ranging from tall and slender to very grotesque and gnarled. As the wet season arrives, their massive swollen trunks store up large quantities of fluid to ensure their survival through the long hot dry season."
– Gloria Loughman

While recovering from an unwelcome but necessary bout of chemotherapy, Gloria turned to quilting. The next ten years found her dabbling in many areas including strip piecing, bargello, fabric dying, and machine embroidery. What had begun as therapy developed into a passion.

In 1996, she began to take courses in design and color as part of a program for a Diploma of Fine Arts. It was then that she began to make art quilts that reflected the Australian landscape. These quilts, using hand dyed or painted fabrics and featuring extensive embroidery highlighting the vivid colors of Australia, have won numerous awards in Australia, the United States, Europe and Japan.

In addition to making quilts, Gloria has been teaching quilting for many years in New Zealand, the United States, the United Kingdom, Europe and Japan as well as Australia. She has also been invited to serve as a judge and has curated exhibitions of Australian quilts in the United States. Her quilts have been featured in a number of magazines, and she is currently writing a book based upon her landscape workshops.

EMPTY NEST-TWO

By Barbara A. Perrin, Pullman, Michigan

83" x 94" (211cm x 239cm) Machine pieced and machine quilted,
based on a pattern by Susan H. Garman

"This quilt has 255 3/8 inch Ohio Stars pieced from reproduction fabric. Each star has 21 pieces of fabric and no paper piecing. It is surrounded with a border of trapuntoed, tapered triangles. Machine quilted with original quilting designs. This is my tenth quilt; from a pattern by Susan H. Garman.

– Barbara Perrin

Barbara first learned to love the feel of a needle in her hand when her grandmother taught her to crochet and knit as a little girl. Although her grandmother didn't quilt, she did instill the love of working with a needle. Barbara finally learned to sew when she was nine years old in 4-H, but she didn't begin quilting until her middle son left home for college in 1995. Since then, quilting has taken over her life.

This quilt, which took her over a year to complete, has won many prizes including a first place at the 2001 Indiana Heritage Quilt show where it competed against another of Barbara's quilts which placed second.

This year's IQA show was especially exciting for Barbara as her *Turkish Treasures - A Red Rendition* was also a winner. For a view of that quilt, see page 62.

LOVE FOR BALTIMORE ALBUM QUILT

By Megumi Mizuno, Shiki City, Saitama Prefect, Japan

80" x 80" (205cm x 205cm) Hand pieced, appliquéd and quilted

I have always thought the Baltimore Album quilt is the supreme form of beauty, and it was my dream to make one myself, for once in my lifetime. It took me almost three years to make this piece. It took many trials to make a block. It was a long, joyful journey in quest for seeds of beauty – I looked for inspiration in books of patchwork, books of gardening, and even in my own garden!
– Megumi Mizuno

A knitter and dressmaker, Megumi Mizuno certainly wasn't planning to become a quilter when, in 1987, she stopped at the craft department at a local department store. The store, however, was offering a free class on quilt-making to anyone who would purchase quilting materials at the store. She thought that the bag displayed there was so lovely that she signed up for the class.

Today she describes herself as a professional quilter and quilt lecturer. Married to a banker, she is the mother of a daughter who is a university student, but most of her time seems to be occupied with quiltmaking. Her prize-winning quilt took her more than three years to complete.

Besides winning an award in the IQA competition, *Love for Baltimore Album Quilt* won the Premium Prize in the International Great Quilt Festival in Tokyo. Her *Rose and Sampler* was honored in the 2002 International Great Quilt Festival in Tokyo.

Megumi Mizuno finds tremendous joy in the process of cutting a large piece of cloth, of putting different colors and shapes together to finally create her image of a quilt. Her happiest moments are spent making quilts. The winning of this award in the IQA competition is a great incentive for her to continue making beautiful quilts.

FABRIC FOLIAGE

By Helen Giddens, Oklahoma City, Oklahoma

114" x 65" (290cm x 165cm) Machine pieced and machine quilted

"This is the second of my quilts based on actual fabric swatches. Little pieces of print fabric were blown up into a large version for a quilt."
– Helen Giddens

When Helen Giddens's grandmother presented her parents with a pink, black and white *New York Beauty* quilt, she couldn't have known this gift would inspire her granddaughter to become a lifelong and acclaimed quilting artist. Quilting since the age of 16, Helen's quiltmaking hobby has become her artistic passion and her quilts have been honored in competitions throughout the United States.

Helen's quilt *Treasures* won the 1989 Texas State Memories of Childhood contest; and her *Spook Alarm* won First Place in the Art, Machine Quilted category at Quilts, a World of Beauty. She has been included in Quilt National in 1989 for *Armadillo Highway* and in 1991 for *Wash-Day Whirls*. Her quilt *Snake* is included in the James's Contemporary Quilt Collection and was nominated in the Ultimate Quilt Search for the Twentieth Century's 100 Best American Quilts. Helen's quilts have also been honored at the Dallas Quilt Celebration, Quilter's Heritage, AQS and many more.

Helen Giddens makes all of her quilts from scrap fabric or fabric "gifts" as she calls them. She spent about 1 1/2 months actually making her IQA award-winning quilt *Fabric Foliage,* but spent a longer period of time collecting the fabric and designing the quilt. Her quilts are her own artistic creations composed of shape, movement, color and personal expression. Although, Helen describes her sewing machine as a "plain Jane" household machine, the artistry that she produces is anything but "plain Jane!"

A FINE ROMANCE

By Janet Steadman, Clinton, Washington

40" x 59" (102cm x 150cm) Machine pieced and machine and hand quilted

"Candlelight, wine, and flames in a fireplace could be the start of a fine romance."
– Janet Steadman

For Janet Steadman quilting began in an odd way. In 1983, she became the anxious owner of a seven-foot round bed. In order to make bedding for this huge bed, she found that she would have to learn to quilt. The quilt she made for that bed, which was 120" across, was later to appear at the 1988 IQA show. Now over 20 years and over 80 quilts later, Janet has become a full-time quilt artist, teacher and lecturer.

Working with fabric has become a major part of her life. She remembers as a child stitching bits of colorful fabric together. This love of color and fabric, she feels, is what paved the way for her to become a quilter. She finds that using fabric to communicate helps her talk to others.

Three of her quilts were accepted and displayed in Quilt National exhibits. In addition, her quilts have won top awards in IQA shows. Her quilts have been included in many national and international exhibits, collections and publications.

She and her husband moved back to Washington State from Houston in 1991. They live on Whidbey Island, north of Seattle where she works from her home studio which offers a fantastic view of Puget Sound.

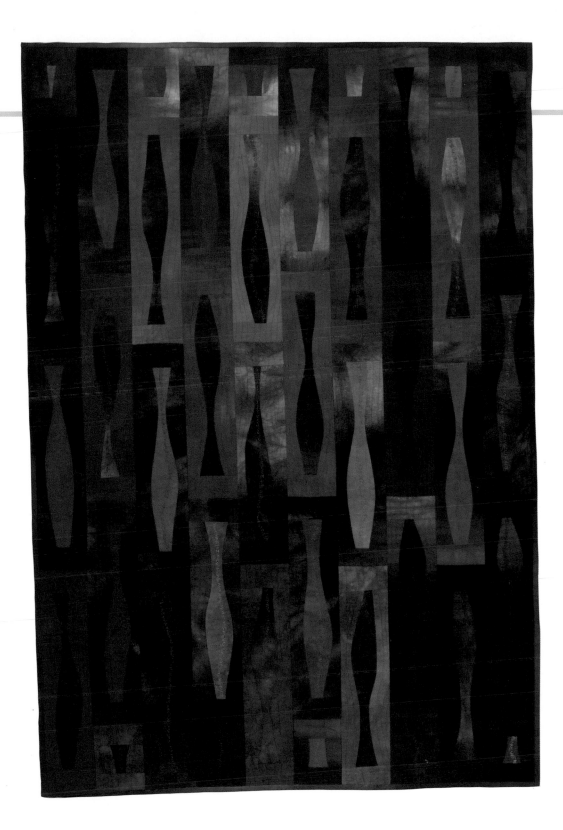

CHOPSTICK CHALLENGE

By Patrice Perkins Creswell, Austin, Texas

74" x 74" (188cm x 188cm) Machine and hand pieced
and machine and hand quilted

"This quilt is a lighthearted tribute to my problems with chopsticks. I love the concept, but mastery is an ongoing challenge."
– Patrice Perkins Creswell

While Patrice was in college preparing to become a registered nurse, she tried a little quilting. This interest continued as she married and raised her three children. She was always interested in various patterns, and initially she was completely self-taught.

Eventually the quilting bug bit, and quilting took over Patrice's life. Today in addition to making her own quilts, she works in a quilt shop where she teaches others to enjoy her love of quilting.

While she enjoys playing the piano and gardening, quiltmaking occupies much of her time. This prize-winning quilt took her about eight months to complete.

Other of her quilts have won prizes, including her *Crewel Whirl* and *Carmen's Veranda,* which both won category first prizes in previous IQA competitions.

MAPLE BREAKS

By Gabrielle Swain, Watauga, Texas

*"My work continues to explore
our impact on nature...
and how separate we are
from nature."*
– Gabrielle Swain

50" x 36" (127cm x 86cm) Machine pieced and hand quilted

In 1983, Gabrielle – with three small children – retired from her career directing, acting and managing regional theatres. She began searching for other creative endeavors. Because her mother-in-law had always wanted to learn to make a quilt, Gabrielle thought this experience might provide something for the two of them to do together.

Gabrielle didn't find quilting; quilting found her. Now, many years later, she describes herself as a quiltmaker, author, teacher and lecturer. Quiltmaking has become not only her profession but also her passion!

Her quilts, which take from six to nine months to complete, have won prizes including Best Hand Workmanship for Wall Quilts in the 2000 American Quilters Society competition and the Best of Show Wall Quilt Award in 2003 from the American Quilters Society.

Gabrielle insists that there is no better activity to get involved with than the making of quilts and no better place than her studio. Her wish for everyone is to find that place of passion, as she has with quiltmaking, in some aspect of our lives.

For another quilt by Gabrielle Swain, see page 104.

LEAVES IN LIVING COLOR
By Libby Lehman, Houston, Texas

"I used one of the design techniques from my class, Creativity for Klutzes. For once, I practiced what I preached!"
– Libby Lehman

54" x 73" (137cm x 185cm) Machine pieced and quilted

Libby Lehman began quiltmaking in 1971 when her mother Catherine Anthony enrolled the two of them in a basic quilting class. Libby has always been thankful that they share this love of quilting which they learned as adults and peers rather than as mother and child.

After this basic class, mother and daughter bought every book they could find on quilting and began making traditional quilts. Eventually Catherine and several of her friends opened a quilt shop in Houston, and Libby began teaching in the shop. It was, however, when Catherine brought innovative teachers like Nancy Crow, Michael James and Nancy Halpern to the shop that Libby began making contemporary art type quilts.

Today, over thirty years later, Libby Lehman is an internationally renowned art quiltmaker whose works appear in many private, corporate and museum collections. She teaches extensively in the United States as well as Australia, New Zealand, Japan, Germany and Switzerland. Over the years she has evolved from a traditional hand worker into one of the leaders in innovative machine stitchery. The unique look of her quilts stems from her use of the sheer ribbon illusion that creates the appearance of translucence on her quilts.

Many of her quilts have won honors including *Escapade,* which won a first place in the AQS show and *Captive Color,* which won a first place ribbon at an IQA show. *Power of Houston,* which she created with two other quiltmakers, won first place in the Group Quilt Category in the 2000 IQA show. Her *Joy Ride,* which expresses the joy Libby gets out of quilt making, was selected as one of the Twentieth Century's 100 Best American Quilts.

DOUBLE DUENDE

By Lonni Rossi, Wynnewood, Pennsylvania

"The Spanish poet, Federico Garcia Lorca, once gave a lecture about what he called the Andalusian 'spirit of creativity' – the Duende – which has captivated my attention for the past few years. Starting with an offset print of two large leaves on white fabric, parts of the wholecloth background were then silk-screened, stamped, stenciled and eventually, over-painted, to emphasize the concept. Extensive machine embroidery, couching, and quilting over fused fabric pieces were then added to bring out more texture as well as the 'other worldly' effect of two souls in search of their own creative paths."

– Lonni Rossi

65" x 40" (165cm x 102cm) Machine pieced and machine quilted

A professional graphic designer for over thirty years, known for her work in corporate identity, logo design, packaging design and state-of-the-art typography, Lonni Rossi has won numerous design industry awards.

In 1987, searching for a more personal form of expression in addition to the world of graphic design, she discovered fiber art and quiltmaking. She became especially intrigued with Amish quilts and started experimenting with graphic designs in cloth. Today, after 17 years as a serious maker of art quilts, the medium has become her primary creative focus.

She likes to create her own hand painted fabrics, which combine her love of communications through typographic design and the written word with textiles and quiltmaking. Beginning with white fabric as her blank canvas, she achieves surface texture on the fabric using her original designs in combination with silk screening, stenciling, rubber stamping and hand painting. These one-of-kind fabrics are then used in combination with extensive machine embroidery and quilting to create her award winning art quilts.

Her *Cabins in the Cosmos* won Best Wall Quilt in the 1999 AQS Show, and her *My Mind's in a Tangle* was a Judge's Choice Award in the IQA 1999 show and won the Most Innovative Quilt Award in the 2000 Schweinfurth Art Museum show.

Today in addition to her quiltmaking, Lonni designs fabric for Andover Fabrics and operates her own graphic communications company

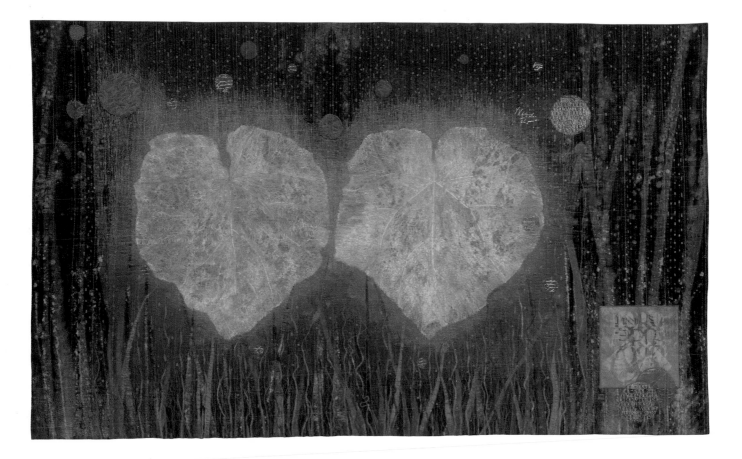

THE WILD GARDEN – ECHINACEA

By Rita Steffenson, Edwards, California

87" x 61" (221cm x 155cm)
Machine pieced and machine quilted

"My joy of gardening and the sight of this stunning bush inspired me to create this quilt. The elements were sketched individually from my photos and then combined to create this composition. I hand dyed the fabrics with my color mixtures to achieve the natural color palette. The quilting line creates texture that makes this work come alive. 'The Wild Garden' series represents a fragment of the abundant free beauty nature provides."

– Rita Steffenson

In 1992, after the birth of her third child, Rita left her job as an environmental analyst to stay home and raise her children. Her husband, an officer in the United States Air Force, was often away for weeks at a time, and Rita needed a challenge to break up the routine of household chores. Although she had never sewn before and didn't have any quilters in her family, she decided that it would be a simple task to make a few small quilts for her children.

The first few attempts were frustrating. The quilts looked fairly simple on graph paper; the math was easy, but the construction was difficult — especially getting the sewing machine to co-operate. Rita insists that she made more mistakes than she can remember, but she kept at it, determined not to let quiltmaking defeat her. Eventually Rita joined a quilt guild and began attending quilt shows. She began to grasp the possibilities that were open to her by creating art quilts. The knowledge that she gained from doing things the wrong way first and then finding solutions through troubleshooting gave her a unique set of skills to draw upon once she started making art quilts.

This prize-winning quilt took her one year to design, over five months to actually construct and over 250 hours to quilt. Her quilts have won many prizes including awards at both the AQS and Road to California Shows for her *The Wild Garden – Sundown.*

A MINIATURE ROSE GARDEN FOR JESSIE

By Martha A. Nordstrand, San Diego, California

16" x 16" (41cm x 41cm) Hand appliquéd and hand quilted

*"In memory of Jessie Harrison,
who was a friend and a true
miniature artist. Each rose
is based on a variety of
miniature roses."*
– Martha Nordstrand

Martha was born in the deep South to a family of needleworkers and quilters. While she often says that she was born with a needle in her hand, the truth is that her grandmother placed it there when she was three. Her grandmother made quilts for the love of the art and to provide coverings for beds. Martha can't ever remember sleeping under "store bought" blankets. Some of her happiest childhood memories are the hours she spent with Grandma's scrap bag in the closet, cutting and stitching little dresses and quilts for her dolls.

Years later Martha graduated from college with a major in art. She tried knitting, crocheting, embroidery and needlework, but always seemed drawn to fabrics and textiles; her closet of fabrics was proof of this fact. She made simple quilts for her daughter and baby quilts for friends until she realized that she had made a complete circle back to where she started in her grandmother's scrap bag. She then began quilting in earnest.

In addition to quilting, Martha loves gardening and flowers, and was, therefore, drawn to appliqué where she could plant her flowers on her quilts. Not satisfied with the traditional methods of appliqué, Martha proceeded to develop her own method which allows her to create the realistic flowers that appear in her quilts.

Most of her quilts are memorials made for many of the important people in her life who have supported and given her encouragement over the years.

LE JARDIN AZURE

*By Myrl Lehman Tapungot, Pio Taneo, Jr., Vergie Joven,
Jun Joven, Alvira Morandante,
Tata Maagad and Luz Macabata,
Cagayan De Oro City, Mindanao, Phillipines*

80" x 83" (203cm x 211cm) Hand pieced, hand appliquéd,
beaded and hand quilted

"Three fantastical mermaids float above impossible depths of blueness with mystical living treasures amid the warm coursing liquid of life. Intermingling with my boundless, ceaseless imagination it forms a living dream, bonding fantasy and reality in the azure world below, with its whimsical delights, hidden discoveries, and the timelessness of the wandering mind."
– Myrl Lehman Tapungot

Unlike most groups who submit quilts in competitions, these quilters are employees of M. Deans House of Design. This is a small family business that started in 1984 in Cagayan De Oro City on the Island of Mindanao in the Philippines. The company employs about 150 people who make the quilts – all by hand.

The quilting is done using traditional methods in the employees' own homes, providing scores of families in the area with additional income and stability. This also affords the quilters a chance to earn income while caring for their homes and families. Many of the quilters' main source of income is farming, and quilting provides a valuable supplemental income between seasons.

Made of hand-dyed silk and a collection of more than 50 blue cottons, this quilt took over two years to compete. Marl Lehman Tapungot and Pio Taneo, Jr. worked on the design while three people quilted and four others did the appliqué, embroidery and beadwork.

Recently the quilters have begun entering competitions. Usually it is difficult for group quilts to compete because several hands work them and therefore the stitches are often variable. The M. Dean quilters pride themselves on making quilts with perfectly identical stitches.

Enchanted Doorway II won both the Group Quilt category and the Judge's Choice at the 1999 IQA competition. In addition other quilts made by the group have won awards at several AQS competitions, Quilt Yokohama, Pacific International Quilt Festival, and the 1996 and 1995 IQA competitions.

WISH BIRD

By Liuxin Newman, Turramurra, NSW Australia

82" x 90" (208cm x 229cm) Hand quilted

"Inspired by traditional Chinese symbols of hope. The Phoenix is a bird that never dies. Hope for peace and harmony will forever live!"
– Liuxin Newman

In 1995 purely by chance, Liuxin took a book off the shelf in a book shop that had the word "quilting" etched on the jacket. After discovering what the word "quilting" meant, her interest in this new art form was born. She was completely fascinated, and happily "hooked" ever since.

Since she hand quilts, Liuxin became aware of problems that hand quilters encounter. She determined that thimbles currently on the market have small, closely spaced dimples that make it difficult to work. She decided that deeper dimples would help to grasp the needle better. Because she also enjoys silver smithing in addition to quilting, Liuxin soon designed her special thimble. Today her company, Thimblelady, sells her special thimbles throughout the world, and Liuxin travels promoting her "no pain" method of quilting.

Her quilts, including *Four Friends* and *Wish Bird* have both won first prize in quilt competitions in Australia. *Wish Bird* took her nine months to complete.

Liuxin feels that sharing her quilting technique has won her the friendship of many wonderful quilters. Quilting itself, she insists, has taught her how to live a fuller life.

TURKISH TREASURES – A RED RENDITION

By Barbara A. Perrin, Pullman, Michigan

76" x 85" (193cm x 216cm) Machine pieced and machine quilted

"This Boston Commons quilt was inspired by Diane Gaudynski's Red Square wall quilt and the Turkish Treasurers fabric collection from P&B. Quilting designs by Diane Gaudynski are from Choosing Quilting Designs published by Rodale and also some original. My eleventh bed quilt, it is machine quilted and took eight months to make."

– Barbara Perrin

In 1995, Barbara became interested in quilting after watching Harriet Hargrave teach machine quilting on television. She knew instantly that she wanted to learn to quilt and to do so by machine.

The oldest of six children, Barbara was raised on her parents' fruit farm. For the first six years of her education, she attended a one room country school where one teacher taught grades kindergarten through eighth grade. After graduating from college, she married, and she and her husband built their home only one mile from where she had been raised.

Barbara's favorite quilts are antique and traditional quilts. Her pleasure in quilting comes from experiencing the beautiful and recreating it. She especially enjoys heirloom machine quilting and being able to make something special for her children.

This quilt, which took Barbara eight months to complete, has won over $3,000 in awards at quilt shows all over the country.

For a look at Barbara's other quilt which took a top category award at this year's IQA show, see page 38.

FIRST PLACE,
MIXED TECHNIQUE
AWARD SPONSORED BY
QUILTERS' RESOURCE, INC.

AUTUMN IN NEW ENGLAND

By Barbara Barrick McKie, Lyme, Connecticut

81" x 48 1/2" (206cm x 123cm) Machine pieced, disperse dyed polyester computer transfers with free-motion machine quilting

"This quilt pictures scenes that I captured in the autumn of 2000 around my home. The separate images are connected with scanned leaves that I collected on my walks during that time. The colors never cease to inspire me as I look for natural subjects to capture in my work."

– Barbara Barrick McKie

When Barbara and her husband purchased their first home in 1971, she decided to make a quilt for each of the four bedrooms, using her own original design. Since there were very few books on quilting at the time, Barbara's grandmother supplied most of the advice. By the time Barbara had finished the process, she was so enthusiastic about quilting and creating in fabric that she began making quilts for the walls. Eventually she starting making and selling what today are referred to as art quilts.

During the 1980s Barbara returned to work; she was a research microbiologist. With a fairly long commute she had little time for quilting. However, in 1991, she returned to school to earn a master's degree in marketing. Now she found time for quilting, and she was intrigued with the new techniques that had been perfected during the 80s. By 1994 she was again a professional art quilter.

Barbara consolidates her whole life in her art. Her many careers, whether microbiology or computers, are reflected in her art. She has always applied what she knows from one interest and combined it uniquely with something else. Her work has been juried into many national and international shows including being juried as a finalist into every IQA

show since 1996. She was also selected for many highly competitive shows including Quilt National and the American Folk Art Museum in New York where two works were selected for their juried art quilt show, including *Spirit of Design*, which traveled internationally. Twenty-three magazines or books have featured her works.

DON'T WORRY, BE HAPPY

By Cheri Meineke-Johnson, Corinth, Texas and Linda Taylor, Melissa, Texas

"Original design. Batiks and hand-dyed fabrics hand appliquéd to a solid background fabric. Original free-hand machine quilting designed for this quilt. Swarovski crystals heat applied."
– Cheri Meineke-Johnson and Linda Taylor

83 1/2" x 72 1/2" (212cm x 184cm) Hand appliquéd and Machine quilted

Cheri's background is in the automotive business. Her father is the founder of Meineke Car Care (formerly Meineke Discount Mufflers), and Cheri has owned and operated an auto shop since 1979. Today, however, she considers quilting to be her profession,

In 1996, Cheri's mother introduced her to quilting. She lent Cheri a 1950s Singer sewing machine and supplied the fabric from her stash. Because of the 250 miles which separated Cheri and her mother, Cheri considers herself a "phone taught" quilter. The first "quilt call" came when the sewing machine ran out of thread. Having never sewn before, Cheri was at a loss as to how to rethread the machine. This first quilt is still waiting to be finished.

Cheri's second quilt, *Family,* introduced her trademark style: using one fabric, fussy cuts, repeats, the nine degree ruler and circles. When the top was completed, Cheri found out that she was one of those "I do tops; I don't quilt quilts" quilters. That is where the relationship with Linda Taylor began which has resulted in many prize-winning quilts.

Linda and Cheri don't do pre-design work as a team. Cheri does her part, and then drops off the top and walks away. Linda, a talented longarm quilter, then works her magic. It has been said that the two offer a good marriage of styles.

Linda is a highly awarded longarm machine quilter whose work has been displayed in many venues and published in quilting magazines and books. For another prize-winning quilt by Linda, see page 120.

BEYOND COLOR PURPLE

By Jenny Haskins, Castle Hill, NSW Australia

94 1/2" x 94 1/2" (240cm x 240cm) Hand pieced and machine quilted

"This quilt follows on from Color Purple *and* Color Purple Next Generation *to promote and bring recognition to machine embroidered quilting. Original designs & quilt."*
– Jenny Haskins

Passionate about color, Jenny was an artist for years using a variety of media, her favorite being onglaze painting on porcelain, which she taught in her studio for many years. In 1991 she joined the Pfaff Company in Australia as the National Education and Training Manager, later being promoted to National Marketing Manager. In these capacities she promoted the creative world of machine embroidery

In 1999, Jenny formed her own company, Unique Creative Opportunities Pty Limited with her daughter Sam as director and her son Simon as manager. Together they produce books and creative embroidery design disks, many of which are made into quilts. They also lecture, give classes and teach machine embroidery in the United States, Australia, New Zealand and Germany.

She is the author of eight books and has edited five popular machine embroidery magazines. Currently she is the editor of the Australian magazine *Creative Expressions* which focuses on machine embellished quilts and machine embroidery techniques and ideas.

Her passion is machine embellished quilting. Teaching, promoting and extolling the virtues of this fine art occupy most of her energies. This is only the second time that Jenny has entered a quilt competition and the first time she has won an award.

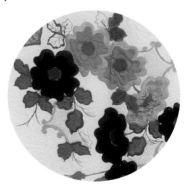

3-D PARTY EXPLOSION

By Cara Gulati, Nicasio, California

"This is the third quilt in a series of 3-D explosion designs that I have developed. It's been so much fun that I'm going to write a book on the technique."
— Cara Gulati

77" x 84" (196cm x 213cm) Machine pieced and machine quilted

In 1992, Cara Gulati was working as a designer of children's wear. She didn't understand what cutting fabric up into little pieces and then sewing them back together was all about. A friend, however, was making quilts, and Cara decided to investigate.

In the years since then, Cara has made over 75 quilts, spends over 20 hours a week quilting, teaches, produces and sells her own line of patterns through her company, Doodle Press, whose motto "Designs that start with a doodle and end up as art" expresses Cara's quilting philosophy.

Cara encourages quilters to loosen up and have fun with their quilting. If you aren't smiling, she feels that it's time to work on something else. According to Cara, not every piece has to be a masterpiece. A mistake is an opportunity to learn something new. Ripping out seams doesn't make you better at sewing seams together correctly.

PUTTING ON THE RITZ

By Gayle Wallace, Taylor, Louisiana

"Jacket was an original adaptation of a commercial pattern. Quilting designs were adaptations of a fabric design. Designs were hand stuffed and hand beaded. Fabric is dupioni silk."

– Gayle Wallace

Machine pieced and machine quilted

Almost twenty years ago, Gayle, who was a professional seamstress, began attending a beginning quilting class as a lark. That "lark" gave her life a new twist; quilting has now become her profession.

Quilting has been the great joy in her life, affording her the opportunity to meet many great new friends through this wonderful art form. According to Gayle, it's better than therapy, and you have something to show for the time and energy you put into your quiltmaking.

In addition to creating quilted garments such as this jacket, Gayle has produced a number of prize-winning quilts including her *Spin Around New York,* which placed in the 2002 IQA show as well as winning best of show at the GSQA show in New Orleans.

Today Gayle is a professional longarm quilter, and her machine quilting has been part of several award winning quilts at the 2002 AQS show and the 2000 NQA show.

Her prize winning jacket took her approximately 250 hours to complete.

2002 QUILTS

FLOWERS OF THE CROWN
By Shirley P. Kelly, Colden, New York

78" x 58" (198cm x 147cm) Hand appliquéd and machine quilted

"After each of the Triple Crown races, a blanket of flowers is draped over the winner: roses at the Derby, black-eyed-susans for the Preakness and carnations to the Belmont victor. The races of 1978 provided three of the most contentious battles of the century with Affirmed prevailing by 7 $^1/_2$ lengths or less. In the Belmont, depicted here, Affirmed and Alydar would run head-to-head over the last mile, with Affirmed winning the Crown and all three blankets of flowers."
– Shirley P. Kelly

Art has always been an important part of Shirley's life; she was a high school art instructor for 33 years. Approximately 20 years ago, however, Shirley began quilting. Today she considers quilting her profession; drawing and photography have become merely hobbies.

Her first quilting project, a toy lamb for her oldest grandchild, was a far cry from the prize-winning quilts that Shirley has since created. In 1996, her *Two Minutes in May* won a first place in the Small Art quilt category at the IQA show and was named as one of the Twentieth Century's 100 Best American Quilts in addition to being honored at many other quilt competitions. Her quilt ...*And Friends of the Family* was awarded the Robert S. Cohan Master Award for Traditional Artistry at the 2001 IQA show .

The National Museum of Racing and Hall of Fame in Saratoga, New York has honored *Flowers of the Crown* by hanging it in the museum in 2004.

Shirley's philosophy is that one never creates a quilt in a vacuum. She feels that the fine quilt teachers she has met in her life have influenced her creatively and technically. In addition beautiful fabrics, both hand-dyed and printed, have also helped provide inspiration for her work.

THE ROEBUCK QUILT REDONE

By Kim McLean, Lindfield, NSW Australia

92" x 92" (234cm x 234cm) Hand pieced and hand quilted

"Inspired by a photo in Historic Australian Quilts by Annette Gero. Annette and I are collaborating on another book of Australian quilts. Annette will cover history, and I'll be writing instructions on how to make the quilts."

– Kim McLean

When Kim McLean took a beginning sampler class in 1990, little did she realize that quilting would become such an important part of her life. It didn't take long for her to become hooked on buying fabrics and the quilting tools needed to fashion quilts.

Today this former pharmacist is busy creating prize winning quilts. This quilt took her a month to draft the pattern and then four to five months of sewing to complete.

In 1991, just one year after she had started quilting, Kim took a Best of Show at the Sydney Quilt Show for her *A Tisket a Tasket Fill Up Casey's Baskets,* which then went on to win an Honorable Mention at the AQS Show in Paducah in 1992.

In 1992, Kim repeated a Best of Show award at the Sydney Quilt Show for her *Casey, Santa, The Beach, It Must Be Christmas.* In 2003, her *Hexagon Stars* took a Second Prize in Traditional Pieced at the IQA show.

Kim's win at the IQA show still remains the most thrilling moment in her quilting life. She still finds it difficult to believe even now.

THE ROBERT S. COHAN
MASTER AWARD FOR
TRADITIONAL ARTISTRY
AWARD SPONSORED BY
RJR FABRICS

TIMELESS BEAUTY

By Jane Anderson, Vinita, Oklahoma

78" x 95" (198cm x 241cm), Hand pieced and hand quilted

"I drafted my own patterns for this New York Beauty variation and used reproduction fabrics and cotton batting to achieve the look of an antique quilt circa 1900."

– Jane Anderson

Jane's first quilt top was hand-pieced when she was ten years old, but she still hasn't found the time to quilt it. Completely self-taught, Jane began making pillows and wall hangings in the early 1980s. In 1986 she finished her first quilt, and she hasn't stopped.

She worked for approximately two years to complete her *Timeless Beauty*, which has been winning prizes everywhere it is shown, including best of show awards at quilt shows in Oklahoma and Missouri. Her *In the Pink* took home an honorable mention in the Traditional Pieced category in the 2003 IQA competition.

Retired from her career after 28 years in the health care field, Jane devotes herself to making quilts and collecting antique sewing tools. She is married to the perfect quilter's husband: he cooks; she quilts. Jane's one complaint is that she didn't start quilting earlier because she has way too many quilts in her head thirsting to get finished.

SPIROGYRA #1

By Caryl Bryer Fallert, Oswego, Illinois

44" x 109" (112cm x 277cm) Hand dyed and painted, machine pieced, machine appliquéd and machine quilted

"This design is an interpretation of a microscopic view of Spirogyra, a single cell organism. The entire quilt is a study in intersecting color and value gradations. All of the fabrics were hand dyed. The checks were made from a black and white stripe, which was over-dyed in rainbow colors. The ovals were quilted in a pebble pattern. The background and the checks were quilted in interlocking organic curves that suggest flowing water or braided fibers."

- Caryl Bryer Fallert

Caryl Bryer Fallert is an internationally recognized award-winning quilt maker. She is especially well known for her use of scintillating colors and multi-level illusions of light and motion as used in her High Tech Tucks quilts and her curved seam designs displayed in her *Corona II: Solar Eclipse,* which was voted one of the Twentieth Century's 100 Best American Quilts.

Caryl, who learned to sew and crochet when she was very young, was always interested in art. Drawing and painting were some of the favorite activities of her youth. Carol's grandmother had made quilts out of necessity, but Carol's mother was proud of the fact that she could afford to buy blankets and didn't need to make quilts. So Caryl, therefore, never learned to quilt as a young girl.

In 1974, Caryl and her husband bought an old farm from a 79-year-old quilt-maker. Carol loved visiting with her, seeing her stacks of quilts. Quilting looked like an interesting thing to try. She ordered a book and began making quilts. By 1983, she had decided that she liked making quilts more than anything else and she gave up painting, stained glass, knitting, dabbling and began focusing on fabric as a medium for expression. She now paints again, but she is painting with dye on the fabrics she uses in her quilts.

Since then Caryl's quilts have won more than fifteen Best of Show awards including three times at the AQS Show in Paducah. Her work can be found in museums, corporate and private collections in 22 states and six foreign countries.

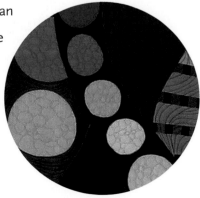

THE PFAFF MASTER AWARD FOR
MACHINE ARTISTRY
AWARD SPONSORED BY
PFAFF SALES AND MARKETING

IN FIELDS OF GOLD

By Diane Gaudynski, Waukesha, Wisconsin

83"x 83" (211cm x 211cm) Machine pieced and machine quilted

"Inspired by the gift of a 'skinny quarter' of red toile de jouy from a friend's trip to Paris, this traditional 4-block quilt adds three more large scale vintage fabrics to make up the four stars. Original quilting designs based on antique Provence, Welsh, English and American quilts. Title reflects lavish formal quilting in the golden background or 'field,' as well as the beauty, grace and courage of Michele Kwan's glorious skating to the music of Sting after losing the 2002 Olympic gold medal."

– Diane Gaudynski

Intrigued by fabrics and designs, Diane taught herself to quilt, initially becoming proficient at hand quilting. After hearing a lecture by Harriet Hargrave and viewing a quilt by Debra Wagner that was machine quilted, she began perfecting her machine quilting. She feels that this quilt reflects years of work perfecting her art so that she can proudly say, "Yes, my quilt is machine quilted." The quilting designs which are original except for the use of Jeanna Kimball's rabbit, are based on antique Provence, Welsh, English and American quilts.

The author of *Guide to Machine Quilting*, Diane won the Pfaff Master Award for her *Through A Glass Darkly: An American Memory* at the 2001 IQA Show. That quilt also took a first place at the 2002 AQS show and won a best of show at the 2002 NQA show. She was named a master quilter by the NQA and is a four-time recipient of the Machine Workmanship Award at the AQS Show in Paducah.

Diane has been teaching quiltmaking techniques for 14 years. She has specialized in ornate, intricate machine quilting of traditional and original feather designs. Many of her students have now won national awards for their quality machine quilting

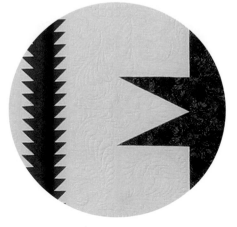

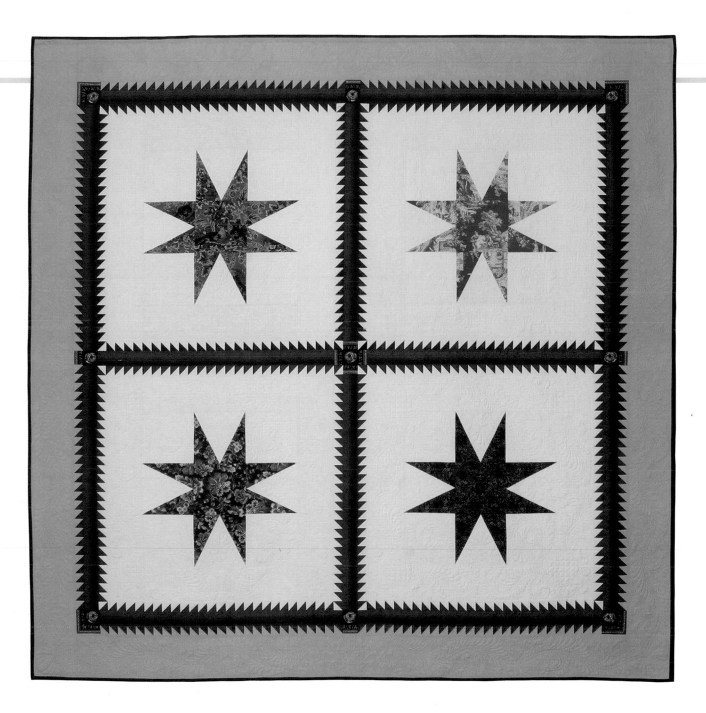

PHARAOH®

By Sandra Frieze Leichner, Albany, Oregon

"This quilt celebrates the art and culture of an ancient Egyptian civilization that continues to capture the imagination in this modern age of technology."
— Sandra Frieze Leichner

76" x 82" (193cm x 208cm) Hand appliquéd, machine pieced and quilted with embroidery and beading

Inspired by an interest in quilt history and a passion for embroidery and design, Sandra Leichner fell in love with hand appliqué, and an award-winning quilter was born. Sandra's quilt *Pharaoh* won the 2003 Best of World award at the World Quilt & Textile Competition as well as the 2002 Best of Show award at the Quilter's Heritage Celebration and the Great Pacific Northwest Quiltfest.

Pharaoh has also won several First Place awards in national and international competitions including the 2003 AQS and the 2002 Mid-Atlantic Quilt Festival. *Grandpa and the Treadle Quilt* won Honorable Mention at the 2001 IQA show, and *American Still Life* won the 2004 Outstanding Large Quilt award at the Road to California Quilter's Showcase.

For this mother of three young children, fine art has been a part of her life since age 16 when she sold her first painting. Her artistic background is evident now that the quilt has become her canvas. Sandra's work reflects an artistic mastery translated to fabric with thread and a traditional quilting style.

THE SEXAGENARY CIRCLE
By Taeko Ohya, Nagasaki-City, Nagasaki, Japan

72 1/2" x 78" (184cm x 198cm) Hand quilted

Fourteen years ago Taeko's husband, a journalist, was transferred to Okinawa. There her young daughter entered kindergarten and began a life as a student. The move to Okinawa changed Taeko's life as well; she began a life as a quilter.

Some of the parents in the school who enjoyed patchwork and quilting formed an interest group, which Taeko joined. She was fascinated to watch the work that was created by moving around the many small bits of cloth. The members of the group quickly became her friends, and her support group started her on the road to becoming a quilter. This new fascination became an important part of her life.

Today with the kindergarten daughter away at the university, Taeko enjoys creating amazing quilts. This prize-winning quilt took only four months to complete and is her first quilt to win a prize in a quilt competition.

GRAVEN IMAGES

By Judy Coates Perez, Austin, Texas

50" x 79" (127cm x 201cm) Hand dyed and machine quilted

"This quilt was inspired by visits to New England cemeteries while doing genealogy research."
– Judy Coates Perez

In 1987, Judy was working in a large architectural design firm doing graphic and environmental design. After designing a mosaic tile dome and several tile paving patterns she started to play with the idea of creating similar designs with fabric and so was born her interest in art quilts.

When she could not find the colors or textures she wanted to use in her work she began painting and dyeing cloth. In many of her earlier quilts she painted images that she machine appliquéd onto pieced hand-dyed cloth. Over the past few years this has evolved into more painted whole cloth work that is machine quilted.

From the very beginning of her quilting, Judy has enjoyed creating images of goddesses, celestial bodies and natural elements. She enjoys exploring spiritual, historical and mythological themes in her work.

Sharing her joy of making art quilts with others has always been an important element in Judy's quilting life. Her quilt group's prize-winning quilt is shown on page 112.

RIVER RUN

By Cassandra Williams, Grants Pass, Oregon

69 1/2" x 37" (177cm x 94cm) Pieced and soft edge appliqué and machine quilted

*"In Oregon our fishermen thrill
to see the seasonal 'run' of
spawning salmon and trout.
Now my fisherman can see
them 'run' year around."*
– Cassandra Williams

An art major in college, Cassandra Williams turned in her oil paints for a new palette of fabrics in 1997 when she began to seriously work on quiltmaking. After first making several bed quilts, she began to devote her quilt time exclusively to art quilts.

She and her husband are both retired and travel four to six months each year. When her husband fishes, Cassandra constructs her next quilt in their recreational vehicle or in a recreation room when one is available. Along the way, Cassandra presents trunk shows and lectures featuring her quilting techniques of raw edge appliqué and free-motion quilting. This prize-winning quilt took six months to complete. She "built" the fish in a trailer in Texas and then quilted the project later at home in Oregon.

Her quilts have won prizes including a third place in the 2002 IQA show for her *Jigsaw Giants,* and a win at the AQS Expo in Nashville for *The Map Makers. River Run* won two awards at the 2002 IQA show, taking both a Judge's Choice award as well as first place for Pictorial Quilts.

FIRST PLACE,
TRADITIONAL PIECED QUILTS
AWARD SPONSORED BY
FROM MARTI MICHELL
(A BRAND NAME OF
MICHELL MARKETING)

GLASS MENAGERIE

By Marla Yeager, Littleton, Colorado

89" x 89" (226cm x 226cm) Machine pieced and machine quilted

*"This quilt was an exercise in
working with hand-dyed and
over-dyed fabrics."*
– Marla Yeager

A present of a Bernina sewing machine for Christmas, 1983 from her new husband, Joe, started Marla Yeager's quilting life. The following year he asked her to make him a quilt and following a set of published instructions, Marla completed her first quilt, a quilt-as-you-go Log Cabin.

Today Marla considers quilting to be her primary hobby as well as her profession. Although she enjoys fly fishing, fly tying and downhill skiing, quilting is still number one with her. Her *Glass Menagerie,* based on the *Cut Glass Dish* block, not only took these honors at the 2002 IQA show but was also honored at the 2002 AQS show. Other of her quilts including *Coronado's Compass, Galaxy Sleigh Ride, The Milky Way* and *Carousel* have been prize winners.

GOLDEN GLOW
By Mildred Sorrells, Macomb, Illinois

88" x 88" (224cm x 224cm) Hand appliquéd, hand embroidered
and hand quilted

"Inspired by an antique quilt that had feathered hearts in the center. The flowers and vines were taken from a Dover book, enlarged, and twisted around to fit areas. Flowers and feathers were embroidered around to make them stand out. The name came from the gold color of the fabrics. When I finished, the quilt just seemed to glow. The hand quilting was difficult because of two thicknesses of Bali fabrics. I used 1200 yards of quilting thread."

– Mildred Sorrells

There is little that Mildred Sorrells hasn't done; she has crocheted, knitted, been a seamstress, dabbled in watercolors, and learned to paint. All of these skills with their incorporation of color, texture, design and precision in workmanship were excellent preparations for the art of quiltmaking.

An ad in *The Farm Journal* magazine for "Let's Make a Patchwork Quilt" started the journey.

She began making one sampler quilt after another until through the years hundreds of quilts from wall hangings to miniatures had come to life. She first concentrated on traditional quilts only but gradually started to produce her own designs, garnering her ideas from all avenues of life.

She teaches regularly at a local quilt shop and for guilds around the country. Her quilts have won awards at the AQS show and at the 1999 IQA competition.

BRILLIANT STAR

By Noriko Kobayashi, Yokohama, Japan

62" x 62" (157cm x 157cm) Hand and machine pieced and hand quilted

"I found the blue cloth and made this quilt, imagining the star that shines with it."
– Noriko Kobayashi

Noriko Kobayashi began quilting 15 years ago. Because quilting is so often a communal affair, she found it a great way to meet and make new friends.

She spent one year working on *Brilliant Star* and it is her first prize-winning quilt. In addition to quilting she also performs the intricate and beautiful Japanese Tea Ceremony.

A quilting success story, Mrs. Kobayashi has undoubtedly made many new friends in her 15 years of quilting. And now, with her quilt *Brilliant Star* as an ambassador, she will have both fans and friends all over the world.

JUNGLE FLOWERS

By Karen Eckmeier, Kent, Connecticut

28" x 33" (71cm x 84cm) Hand painted fabrics, hand and machine appliqué, curved piecing

"In this series of jungle/leaf quilts, I am working with opposites: curved lines/sharp points, darks/lights. The high contrast of positive-negative spaces creates energy and movement. It also symbolizes the extreme highs and lows that we experience in life. We need them both to stay balanced."

– Karen Eckmeier

In 1987, Karen Eckmeier bought a *Star of Bethlehem* quilt in Pennsylvania and fell in love with the fabrics and texture that the hand quilting gave to the surface. She decided to teach herself how to make quilts, but first, she had to teach herself how to thread a sewing machine since she had no sewing background. She had, however, always liked to draw and she had taken art lessons since she was six years old. Karen reasoned that if she could draw it, she could sew it. It took her a while to perfect her sewing skills, but the results are obvious.

Today Karen, who has worked in banking, communications and real estate, is now a professional quilt artist and writer. She works seven days a week on her art quilts; quilting has taken over her life. It may have started as a hobby, but it is now her business. In addition to making prize-winning quilts, Karen has her own pattern business and travels around the country offering workshops and lectures on her "layered curves," an original technique for sewing dramatic curves. She has been a contributing writer to books and magazines.

In addition to appearing at IQA Shows, Karen's quilts have been juried into AQS competitions, the invitational Tokyo International Great Quilt Festival, the Schweinfurth Memorial Art Center Quilt Show, and the invitational Quilted Surface in Germany Show in Oldenburg, Germany.

BOHEMIAN RHAPSODY

By Ricky Tims, Arvada, Colorado

88" x 88" (224cm x 224cm). Machine pieced, appliquéd and quilted

"This quilt began as a small original paper-cut style medallion block. A border was added to create a small wall quilt. Improvising on the theme, the quilt continued to grow. The undulating symmetry is loosely based on a traditional Diamond in a Square. The urns and other appliquéd motifs create large circular effects. The quilt is made from original hand-dyed fabrics and is machine pieced, machine appliquéd, and machine quilted with silk and rayon threads. Ironically, the original medallion from which the quilt emerged was replaced."

– Ricky Tims

If anyone had asked Ricky Tims what he wanted to do when he grew up, quilting would not have been at the bottom of the list; in fact, it would not even had *made* the list. From an early age, Ricky knew that music – not quilting – was to be his life. He recorded his first album at the age of five and was trained at college in concert piano performance and music composition.

But then, quilting found him!

In 1991, working in St. Louis, Missouri as a free-lance music producer afforded him spare time. His grandmother gave Ricky her old electric sewing machine. This sparked his curiosity about sewing, and he decided to make a western shirt. Someone told him that shirts were difficult to make so he decided instead to make a quilt. No one had ever told him that making a quilt could be difficult. That first sampler quilt started Ricky on an amazing road from traditional templates to the creative style he follows today.

Although quilting has invaded his career as a music conductor, composer and producer, he has found a way to utilize both music and quilting in a unique way. His lectures and classes combine his two great loves. The creativity necessary for one feeds and encourages the creativity for the other.

His *Songe d'Automne* won the Pfaff Master Award for Machine Artistry in 2000 as well as awards at other quilt competitions. His *Passage, Time Warp* and *Summer in the City* were juried into prestigious shows in 1999. In 1998, *Passage* appeared on the cover of a CD recording produced by Ricky and performed by the Saint Louis Voices United mixed chorus and the Saint Louis Symphony Orchestra.

ECLIPSE

By Gabrielle Swain, Watauga, Texas

"This is a continuation of a series focusing on autumn and leaves."
– Gabrielle Swain

50" x 40" (127cm x 102cm) Hand appliquéd and hand quilted

Best known for her use of color, Gabrielle Swain began quiltmaking in 1983. Her current work, which has centered on the relationship between herself and nature, is a continuing study of nature. Her quilts range from realistic to abstract.

She is the author of two books on appliqué and has been featured in many publications both national and international. One of the founding members of the North Texas Quilt Artists, she is also a member of the Studio Art Quilt Associates.

For more on Gabrielle Swain and her *Maple Breaks* which won first place in this category of Innovative Appliqué Small, at the 2003 IQA show, see page 48.

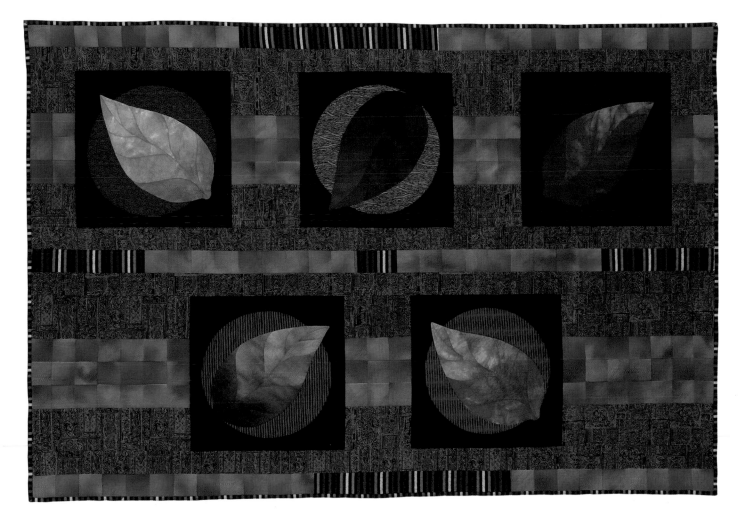

CRESCENDO

By Carol Taylor, Pittsford, New York

67" x 86" (170cm x 218cm) Appliqué, curved piecing and machine quilting

"Often in musical arrangements, the exciting parts are announced in a grand forte after building in intensity from a soft pianissimo. This is called a crescendo. Like a conductor who masterfully builds to the grand finale by punctuating notes and tempo and repeating rhythms, this quilt's subtle fabric placements from light to dark with interspersion of texture heightens the visual excitement."

– Carol Taylor

In 1993, Carol Taylor owned her own business as a sales recruiter, a field she had been working in for almost twenty years. She signed up for a local quilting class which wasn't scheduled to start for two months. Eager to begin, Carol consulted some quilting books and by the time the class had begun, she had made four quilts.

Ten years later, Carol has made over 400 quilts, and has closed her business to devote herself to quilting full time. She began entering competitions in 1998 and has won over 30 top awards including a first at the 2003 AQS show, a win at the 2003 IQA show for *Cymbalism* and eight other prizes at shows in just that year. That year was a banner one for Carol; in addition to her ten wins, she sold 27 of her quilts. Her *Sound Waves* was used as the cover of the Yellow Jackets *Jazz Quarter* CD.

Her quilts, which are distinguished by vibrant colors, striking contrasts and heavy machine quilting and embroidery, have been juried into top shows including Quilt National. Her quilts grace the walls of several companies as well as many private collections.

SUN ON MARTY'S BIKE©

By Jean M. Evans, Medina, Ohio

41" x 74" (104cm x 188cm) Painting, Hand appliqué, and hand quilted

"Playing with the design of the sun and shadows on Marty's bike, I enjoyed the distortion and graphic power of the shapes."
— Jean M. Evans

A week-long snowstorm, some extra fabric and a few old paper quilt patterns turned Jean Evans into a lifelong quilter. Since 1985, her quilts have won awards in competitions from Vermont to Indiana and Houston to Tokyo.

Jean's *May Shadows* won at the AQS show and her *Post Cards to the 21st Century* received 2nd place at the 2001 AQS show and was sent to the Tokyo International Great Quilt Festival. In 1998, *Ladies in Waiting* won 1st place and the Judge's Choice award at the Vermont Quilt Festival, and went on to take 2nd place at the National Quilter's Association.

As a quilting artist, Jean enjoys experimenting with color, texture, large shapes, lines, figures, faces and ordinary objects. She feels that the passion and commitment of today's quilters honors the heritage of their ancestors. Certainly, the many children Jean taught during her 33 years as an art teacher would be proud and inspired to know that her quilting artistry has garnered prizes and praise throughout the world.

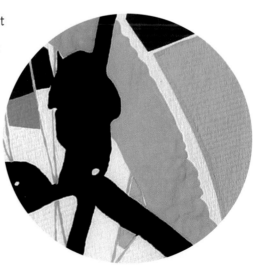

Her *Patio Scene II, Sunday* won the 2003 Fairfield Master Award for Contemporary Artistry and can be seen on page 27.

FEATHERED FANTASY VII

By Mariya Waters, Melbourne, Australia

16 1/2" x 16 1/2" (42cm x 42cm) Machine trapunto and machine quilted

"This is a collection of old feathered wreath and heart patterns on silk satin. It was intended as a full size trapunto quilt, but I decided to see how small I could go."
– Mariya Waters

The international awards Mariya Waters has earned had their gestation at a New Zealand quilt competition in 1990 where her first quilt not only won an award but was included in a book.

Since then Mariya's quilts have won prizes all over the world from the United States to the Netherlands, Great Britain, Japan , France, Germany and Canada. Born in New Zealand and now residing in Australia, Mariya is an old hand at traveling because her husband's employment with an oil company kept the family on the move.

Her quilts are created in three distinct styles: geometric art quilts, innovative pictorial quilts, and traditional quilts enhanced with machine quilting. As an artist her aim is to create innovative quilts using the quilting pattern as part of the design. She also is interested in using patterns drawn from her Maori art heritage

In the 2003 IQA show, both her *Enigma* and her *Dance of the Butterflies* took home awards.

110

FLORA

By Judy Coates Perez , Frances Alford, Yoshiko Kawasaki, Vickie Hallmark, Julie Upshaw, Deb Silva and Sherri Lipman McCauley, Austin, Texas

"This is our fifth group quilt. The theme is based on plant life and things you might find in a garden."
– Judy Coates Perez

32" x 51 1/2" (81cm x 131cm) Hand dyed, hand and machine appliqué, hand and machine quilted

In 1997 a group of quilters from Austin, Texas formed an art quilt group. They began making group quilts, attempting to explore different themes and techniques individually and then bring them together to create a finished quilt. Each member brought different abilities and preferences to the group, but joined for the sole purpose of studying art quilts.

In the beginning they met once a week, spending most meetings working in various mediums doing hands-on projects together. The members feel that these initial experiences are what holds the group together even for members who joined later.

This winning quilt was the fifth in a series of quilts that the group has made together. They chose the theme and then made use of hand-dyed fabric, which they dyed together. Each member was invited to make as many pieces as she wished in four inch multiples, using any technique and in her own style. The group then decided the special arrangement for the blocks, which were attached by fused strips on the back and zig-zag stitching over the raw edges.

When the group began working together, the members lived in Austin and met in person. Since that time several members have moved away, and new ones have joined so the membership now literally stretches from Maine to California. The members, however,

know each other's work so well that all they need is a

theme and fabrics to create prize-winning work.

SHIPPO

By Fusako Nakamura, Toin Chyo, Mie-Ken, Japan

82 1/2" x 96" (210cm x 244cm) Hand appliquéd, pieced and quilted

"I like old-style American quilts and was inspired to make this quilt. The design comes from nature and feelings in my heart."
- Fusako Nakamura

Fusako Nakamura had studied homemaking in school, where her favorite assignments were sewing and making clothes. So, in 1988, after coming across a picture of a beautiful quilt in an American quilt book, she was inspired to become a quilter. Accidental meetings often lead to life-long career undertakings, and this was the case for Fusako.

Today her quilts have won top awards at the International Quilt Week in Yokohama in 2000 and 2002, and at the AQS show in 2002.

The mother of two grown children, Fusako worked on this prize-winning quilt for more than two years. In addition to quilt making, Fusako works on drawing and Japanese calligraphy. Her wins have encouraged her to make even more beautiful quilts.

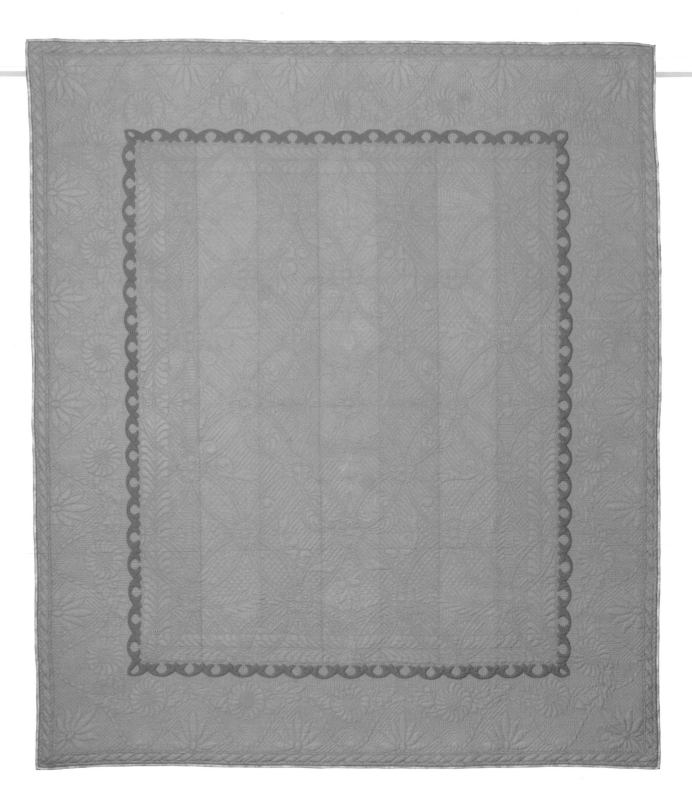

REMEMBERING YESTERDAY...CELEBRATING TODAY

By Jean Lohmar, Galesburg, Illinois

88 1/2" x 88 1/2" (225cm x 225cm) Machine trapunto, machine quilting

"The idea for this quilt began when we started to think about celebrating our fiftieth wedding anniversary, thus the title. The basic design is from an old embroidered homespun bed cover. I enlarged the center and added the second larger chain. Around this circle I placed our wedding date at the top and the anniversary date at the bottom along with the other two quotes about love. The lower right corner has two birds embroidered with our initials. It is white cotton sateen quilted with white silk thread."

– Jean Lohmar

Jean Lohmar made her first quilt over 50 years ago. She had always sewn her own clothing and was fascinated by fiber arts. She had dabbled with crochet, knitting, tatting and embroidery so when she came upon some cross stitch quilt kits in a local department store, she was intrigued.

Eventually quilting became more than just a hobby, and Jean worked in a local sewing machine shop teaching for more than 20 years. Today in addition to making quilts, Jean lectures and teaches machine quilting techniques to guilds and in area shops.

It took Jean more than one and one half years before she was happy with the design and completion of this quilt. While working on the quilt, she reflected on the 50 years she watched her family grow and take their places in society. During those years, it was expected and natural to feel safe; that was changed after 9/11. Working on this quilt during the week of 9/11 helped her to find the feeling of peace and security which she embedded in the quilt to pass on as a legacy to her seven children and her grandchildren.

BERKSHIRE BLISS

By Linda M. Roy, Pittsfield, Massachusetts

"This quilt represents a particularly gorgeous area of our country, as we currently live in the heart of the Berkshires, in western Massachusetts. The autumn colors are spectacular just as the sun fades on a clear day."

— Linda Roy

86" x 86" (218cm x 218cm) Machine pieced, hand appliqué, hand embroidered, hand quilted

Linda Roy began quilting in 1990, when the award-winning quilter, Irma Gail Hatcher, became her neighbor and friend. Since that time Linda has also become a prize-winning quilter. Her *Corinthian Quad* took a top award at both the 2000 IQA and AQS competitions in addition to winning awards in other competitions.

In creating *Berkshire Bliss,* Linda took a simple form which represents the type of quilt that might have been made for warmth and family use in New England. She then took the liberty of blending her own personal style, adding appliqué in the form of Cathedral Window strips and repeating the shapes again in the bias bar appliqué with a touch of embroidery for enhancement. Linda's final touch was adding lots of quilting including some stippling in the muslin border and in other areas with metallic copper thread.

Linda insists that quilting has truly brought out a passion within her unlike any previous hobby or interest.

SALSA

*By Ady Jensen, Key Largo, Florida and
Linda Taylor, Melissa, Texas*

I was inspired by an Indonesian batik. The bright red and green almost make me dance like salsa music. I love the dramatic contrast between the geometric designs and the curves on the quilting."
— Ady Jensen

94 1/2" x 96 1/2" (240cm x 245cm), Machine pieced and machine quilted

Linda is a highly awarded longarm machine quilter whose work has been displayed in many venues and published in quilting magazines and books. A quilter for over 25 years, she is well known and respected as one of the innovators of the art of longarm machine quilting.

She owns and operates a retreat center for longarm quilters in Melissa, Texas where she teaches her innovative methods to thousands of students from all over the world. She has produced seven how-to videos, five books on long-arm techniques and currently has her own PBS television show, "Linda's Longarm Quilting."

Ady had lived in Texas and was a customer and student of Linda's. When she moved to Florida, Ady began importing fabric and taught classes in embel-lishing the fabric with beads for wearables.

When Ady finished the meticulous piecing of *Salsa*, she determined that only Linda could do the quilting. She flew back to Texas with her quilt and presented it to Linda, whose original plan was to do very traditional quilting with trapunto. Once Linda saw the quilt, however, she decided that the quilt needed something more spectacular. So she made use of neon thread, feathers and ferns. Ady was thrilled with the final results and this spectacular win.

HE'S COME UNDONE

By Linda Gillespie, Battle Creek, Michigan and Rebecca Kelley, Signal Mountain, Tennessee

60" x 80" (152cm x 203cm) Hand appliqué, embroidery, beading, airbrushing, and hand quilting

"A family project. Sisters and quiltmakers, Linda Gillespie and Rebecca Kelley, interpreted this original design by their third sister, Cathy Zanoni, a graphic artist. The challenge was to translate graphic art into a manageable pattern that could be transferred into fabric. The three sisters are hoping to work together in forming a new line of quilt patterns."

– Linda Gillespie and Rebecca Kelley

Linda Gillespie was the first of the sisters to become enchanted with quilting. Her quilt *Kaizen* won a third place and a Judge's Choice at an IQA show. In 1992, Rebecca joined Linda at the IQA show and was smitten by the quilting bug as well.

Although the sisters live far from each other, they each have cottages in Geogian Bay, which is north of Toronto. They spend most of their summers there in a beautiful place, which inspires artistic creation and affords plenty of time for quilting.

This prize-winning quilt was designed by their third sister, who – with the help of Linda – has started a new business designing and producing kits, which produce three-dimensional fabric birds. These kits are now available at local quilt stores. While the sisters often work together, they also produce their own quilts and projects as well. Quilting has given them the opportunity to get to know each other as adults.

In addition to winning the Viewers' Choice Award, *He's Come Undone* won an honorable mention at the 2003 AQS show. Rebecca, who specializes in garments, won both Viewers' Choice and the Bernina Workmanship Award at the AQS show.

MAINBOCHER

By Faye Anderson, Boulder, Colorado

Hand pieced and hand quilted

"An art deco-inspired ensemble named for a fashion designer of that period. A wool dress and jacket with couched decorative threads, Ultrasuede medallions, pieced silk swathes, and Raku beads."
– Faye Anderson

In 1980 Faye Anderson took a sampler class at a quilt shop in Denver and saw how quilting could combine her love of sewing with her background in design. It was the start of a life that would produce award-winning quilts and garments. In addition to producing quilts, Faye teaches quilt related workshops and has served as a judge for both quilts and wearables at such prestigious shows as AQS and IQA.

In 1987, Faye took the Best of Show Award at the AQS Show for her *Spring Winds*. The following year her *My Mother Taught Me to Sew* won the top award for Master Appliqué at the AQS Show and then was chosen as one of the Twentieth Century's 100 Best American Quilts.

Faye loves competitions, and has won many prizes at shows throughout the US and Japan. In addition to winning the Wearable Art Award, Faye's *Nouveau Abecedarian* placed in the Innovative Appliqué category at the 2002 IQA Show. *Dreams* won the 1999 Trailblazer Award at Quilt National; her *Famous Women in Art with Quilting Backgrounds* and *Xanadu* have won top prizes. She has also won other top awards for her wearables.